CW00419225

FIREFIGHTING
in
WORCESTERSHIRE

FIREFIGHTING
in
WORCESTERSHIRE

CLIVE S. SHEARMAN
& BRIAN A.E. CORNISH

TEMPUS

Front cover: Worcester's Leyland Turntable Ladder GXA63 gets to work on the fire at J.C. Baker in Foregate Street, Worcester on 2 June 1966. The appliances are Worcester's EFK151 Dennis F12 PE and Bedford J2 Pump 399SFK. *Berrows Newspapers Archives*

Frontispiece: One of my favorite photographs, which has come to light during the research for this project, shows the Wolseley Siddeley tender and trailer pump of the Evesham and Pershore Joint Fire Brigade on Coronation Day 1937. The machine is just passing The Three Tunn's Hotel in Bridge Street, Pershore. *George Hitchcock collection*

First published 2004

Tempus Publishing Limited
The Mill, Brimscombe Port,
Stroud, Gloucestershire, GL5 2QG
www.tempus-publishing.com

© Clive S. Shearman & Brian A.E. Cornish, 2004

The right of Clive S. Shearman & Brian A.E. Cornish to be identified as the Authors of this work has been asserted in accordance with the Copyrights, Designs and Patents Act 1988.

All rights reserved. No part of this book may be reprinted or reproduced or utilised in any form or by any electronic, mechanical or other means, now known or hereafter invented, including photocopying and recording, or in any information storage or retrieval system, without the permission in writing from the Publishers.

British Library Cataloguing in Publication Data.
A catalogue record for this book is available from the British Library.

ISBN 0 7524 3166 8

Typesetting and origination by Tempus Publishing Limited.
Printed in Great Britain.

Contents

Acknowledgements

Obtaining the comprehensive information required for this publication has been a major task. We do not profess it to be complete, but we have attempted to make it as accurate as possible. Therefore we would welcome any additional information and photographic material which would help in making the record of firefighting in Worcestershire complete. The authors can be contacted on 01905 776738 or 01905 778451 or Clive Shearman can be contacted via email at Clive.Shearman18@tesco.net.

We are grateful for the invaluable assistance of a number of people in the preparation of this publication:

D/O Don Oliver, ex-Halesowen and Worcester and West Midlands FS

S/O Gordon Chamberlain, ex-Hereford & Worcester

S/O Alan Davies, ex-Worcester

S/O David Williams, Kidderminster and Worcester

S/O George Hitchcock, ex-Evesham and Pershore RDC and JFB, ex-Redditch

The late S/O Charles Wooldridge, ex-Kidderminster

Sub/O Jim Wall, ex-Malvern

Sub/O Bill Elderkin, ex-Malvern

Sub/O Brian Parsons, Broadway

Sub/O 'Mel' Grinnell, ex-Pershore

Sub/O 'Monty' Wild, ex-Droitwich

Sub/O Vince Davis, ex-Upton-upon-Severn

Sub/O Mel Turbutt, Evesham

Sub/O John Power BEM, ex-Pebworth

Sub/O Clive Allen, ex-Bromsgrove

Sub/O Tom Walker, ex-StourportonSevern

Sub/O 'Pip' Potter, StourportonSevern

Sub/O Paul Gittins, ex-Bewdley

Sub/O 'Mac' Eaton, Redditch and Fire Prevention Bromsgrove

L/Fm George Harris, ex-Droitwich

Fm the late Reg Hartland, ex-Tenbury Wells and Worcester

Fm Ken Edwards, ex-Worcester

Fm Alan Barton, ex-Worcester

Mr Colin Watmore, Hereford & Worcester Fire Brigade Media and Design

Mr Bill Hickin, Millwall, London

Mr Mike Grundy, Memory Lane and Berrows Newspapers

Mr Nigel Smith, Hereford & Worcester Fire Brigade Workshops

Mr M. Print, Secretary of the Pensioners Association

Mr Peter Bowler, former Conservative Redditch Council

Mr Philip Davis, Redditch Library

Mr Paul Walker, Editor, *Redditch Advertiser*

Mr Les Sherlock, Bridgnorth, Shropshire

Dr Terry Daniels, Smethwick, West Midlands

Dr Chris Tallents, Highley FSPG

Mrs Phyllis Hunt, Malvern,Worcestershire

Miss Sarah Probert, Berrows Newspapers, *Evening News,* Library Department

Miss Sheree J., Leeds, Curator of the Norwich Union Insurance Company

Miss Lavender Beard, Upton-upon-Severn Museum

Miss Hebden, Malvern Museum

The staff of the Almonary Museum, Evesham

Foreword

Firefighting in Worcestershire will be of great interest to members of the service, both past and present, and also members of the public and local historians. The authors have clearly spent much time gathering and recording such a wealth of information. I am absolutely certain readers will find a fascinating and unfolding story.

The organisation of the Fire Service is laced with industry and commerce as well as its technical growth. While *Firefighting in Worcestershire* includes an essential section on the National Fire Service, recalling the war years, the story flows well within those years. The book will also be a lasting record of undaunting service to the community of Worcestershire.

In reading, I found myself remembering how much of my life had been lived in the Fire Service. Certain members who will read this book will no doubt recall all their memories. This book can never be considered a dull chronicle of events – it is a readable history and will give pleasure to all who know the Fire Service. Everyone will find pages of great interest and perhaps understanding of the firefighters and their lives. Between the pages, the facts and the pictures, there lies tradition, pride and a noble history.

Sir Reginald Doyle CBE, FIFire, CBIM

Ron Henderson painted this superb watercolour of the Leyland FKT2 Pump Escape of Redditch Fire Brigade.

Introduction

My lifelong interest in firefighting has always led me to want to write a history of the local brigades of the County of Worcestershire. I do not think you realise what is involved in a project like this until you start researching and visiting libraries, local history centres and newspaper archives; then you find to your horror how much history has, literally, been dumped. It may have been accidental or out of ignorance but it is always history that is the loser.

I have been very lucky to have had superb support in this project from Brian Cornish, who has been inspirational in digging up many items which would otherwise have been forgotten. We have spent many hours on the 'phone setting up visits and interviews of former members of the brigade and through this project we have become good friends.

Another person who deserves a special mention is Jim Wall who loaned, over many months, a complete set of Gerald Eastham's reports of the Worcester City and County Fire Brigade and these have proved invaluable in making the book as accurate as possible. But we have made a start which hopefully will be expanded on in the future.

one

The First
Volunteers

From earliest times Worcestershire, like anywhere else, has suffered from the ravages of fire. Early records show that there was a provision made by the Dean of Worcester Cathedral 'to buy twenty buckets and a spout to be ready in any exigency of fire'. Records show that the cathedral suffered destructive fires as early as the eleventh century and that in 1751 a fire nearly destroyed the collection at the Cathedral library. Books dating back 1,000 years stored in the vestry had to be saved after a fire was discovered and several fire engines fought the blaze. This is the first mention of actual fire appliances.

Following the Great Fire of London in 1666, Parliament decreed that every parish should maintain a fire engine, but like today everything that Parliament says is not necessarily done!

In 1708 an Act of Parliament empowered all churchwardens to ensure that stop-blocks and fire cocks were fixed to all water works pipes, and a fire mark made on the front of any house where an instrument was to be kept to open a plug when a fire occurred. A penalty of £10 was levied for failure to comply. In 1709 there is reference to an engine serving the Borough of Bewdley.

The first reference to apparatus for firefighting in Bromsgrove is in 1684 when fire hooks and ladders were bought by the town. By 1700 they had their first engine kept at the Strand, which was manned by constables. By 1822 Bromsgrove had purchased another manual to replace the earlier model. Later the Norwich Union Fire Office presented a manual to the town. In 1846 Bromsgrove Town assumed control of the brigade under their first Captain W. Brown Jnr. He was initially very busy with numerous fires but had to resign shortly after taking office. The Birmingham Fire Office presented Bromsgrove with a former Dudley manual in 1863 to supplement their equipment.

In 1790 records show that Worcester Fire Insurance Co had an office in the city. This is the earliest recorded organised presence. In 1807 an advertisement showed the office as having 'firemen and engines'. In 1818 the business of the Worcester Fire Insurance office was transferred to the Phoenix Fire office in Worcester. In 1840 the Birmingham Fire Office had an engine house at the end of Walsgraves Almshouses next to the Powick Lane entrance to Lady Huntingdon's church.

The Kidderminster Corporation did not possess a fire engine in the early 1800s, but relied on the Assurance companies for cover. In 1841 the Birmingham Fire Office kept one in the market gates in Oxford Road and in 1845 the Royal Farmers Assurance Company kept one at the same location.

A Worcester Fire Office Mark c.1800s. Don
Oliver collection

On Christmas Day in 1844 a ferocious fire occurred at Hartlebury Castle near
Kidderminster. Manuals from Kidderminster, Bromsgrove and Stourport-on-Severn
fought the blaze. Another major outbreak was at the tannery of Henry Beakbane
Ltd, Kidderminster, in 1861, which was nearly destroyed, only to be rebuilt and
then destroyed again a century later. (see Worcester City and County Fire Brigade
9 July 1964).

The Birmingham Fire Office formed a brigade in Redditch in 1841 with one
manual looked after by the local stationer, Mr Bolton. In 1855 Captain W.
Hemming succeeded him. He was also a stationer and went on to found the
Redditch Indicator. By 1868 Redditch had a purpose-built station in Easemore Lane.
In 1873 they purchased a Merryweather fire escape which was kept at the police
station in Evesham Street. By 1876 they were owned by the Lancashire Life and
Insurance Company and were operating two manuals, one of which was named *The
Baron*. In 1881 they moved their base to Alcester Street/Park Road where in 1883
H.C. Browning became the new Captain. In 1892 the Redditch Volunteer Fire
Brigade was formed under new Captain John Kendrick, with a Lieutenant and six
firemen operating two manuals.

The Norwich Union Insurance Company established its brigade in Worcester in
May 1857. They ran a manual engine named *Niagara* in Angel Place. In December
of the same year they added a second machine. Due to a number of incendiary
attacks within the city this prompted a rethink in the positioning of the appliances
and *Niagara* was stationed away from Angel Place.

From 1857-1878 the brigade was commanded by Captain A.P. Watkins. In 1878
Captain Sayce took charge and moulded the Norwich Union Insurance Brigade
into one of the best private outfits in the country. He held office well into the next
century.

Above and below: *Redditch Volunteer Fire Brigade c.1900 outside the Park Road Station and with the team ready harnessed for the shout!* 'Mac' Eaton collection

From its first days the Norwich Union brigade have answered calls locally and as far away as Kidderminster .

In desperate times Worcester was also fortunate to be able to call on the assistance of another of the city's big employers, Cadburys of Blackpole, who ran a horse-drawn manual.

Norwich Union Fire Brigade in Worcester has attended some major fires through the years. The Worcester Music Hall was ravaged by fire in December 1881 and the original theatre burnt down on 24 November 1877, only for its replacement to suffer the same fate on 18 February 1912. (An interesting note on this fire was that the attending support appliances were from the City Police and a local workhouse brigade, believed to be that of the Poor Law Institution in St Paul's, Tallow Hill). All these buildings were covered by policies issued by the Norwich Union.

The first reference to police constables tackling a fire in Worcester was in 1838 in Mealcheapen Street. At that time the police were only asked to assist the local insurance fire crews but by 1840 two sergeants were nominated to learn how to turn the water pipes on and off and a set of keys were then kept at the police station. In 1847 a Wivells fire escape was purchased at a cost of £65. This was stationed at the Old Sheep Market in Angel Place before being transferred to the police station in St Nicholas Street. The policemen became familiar with the escape after regular practice. In 1850 Chief Constable Power reported that:

> The hose stored in St Johns was perished and leaked once water was put through it and it was also far too short to reach the frontages of a considerable amount of properties. On inspection the ladder was also found to be unsafe.

The hose cart with a Worcester City Police Sergeant. Berrows Newspapers

The Copenhagen Street Police Station was opened in 1841 and was the base for the City Police for the next 100 years. The station is situated directly across the street from the main Fire Station and next to the recently vacated former Police Station, which has moved to Castle Street, ironically now opposite the old County Police Headquarters. Clive S. Shearman collection

In 1862 the watch committee called a meeting of all the local insurance companies. Those present were the Royal County, Birmingham District, Birmingham, Fire Co., Sun, Law Union, Royal Exchange, Imperial, Alliance, Phoenix, Norwich Union and Lancashire. Most of those present just provided fire offices within the city while others maintained a brigade. The meeting was intended to form a city fire brigade, but due to disagreements over finance they could not come to a decision. This poor state of affairs would continue to dog the watch committee. During 1871 Chief Constable Power designed and patented a wheeled fire truck to carry ladders and new hose because at this time there were 370 fire-plugs strategically placed around the city for firefighting use.

In 1875 the watch committee called a meeting of all the local insurance companies due to a spate of arson attacks around the city. They agreed to provide equipment and manpower to assist the police under the command of Chief Constable Power while still maintaining separate brigades themselves. This arrangement would last until 1893.

In 1890 the watch committee called a meeting where they decided on a set of rules and equipment required:

1 Police should be primarily responsible for fires.
2 1 Inspector, 2 Sergeants, 12 Constables selected to form brigade.
3 Apparatus required would include a steamer, lengths of hose, hose tender, standpipes and branches, uniform and a hose drying tower.

Captain Breakspeare and the men of the Kidderminster Fire Brigade proudly pose in the rear yard of the old Police Station c.1896. The Kidderminster Shuttle/Times & News

This superb shot of the Shand Mason Steamer (c.1900s) shows it standing at the rear of the Town hall in Vicar Street, Kidderminster, ready to be harnessed up to a team. C. Wooldridge collection

Above and opposite: *The Pike Mills showing the devastation of the previous night's fire: the collapsed gable end, and in the photograph above, the machinery hanging from where the floors used to be.* C. Wooldridge collection

4 All members should reside at or near the police station. All houses to have electric alarms.
5 Four horses to haul the steamer.
6 All large water mains to have hydrants 100-150yds apart. All firemen to have a book of these locations.

The Fire Insurance Offices would bear the cost of these introductions in relation to the size of their risk. Due to the Police Act 1890, the Home Office ruled that any police officer injured or killed on firefighting duties would not be entitled to a pension. The local watch committee decided to take out insurance cover for its policemen for firefighting duties at an estimated £2 per annum, which was quite a bold step at the time. However, in the Police Act 1893 the government made provision for pensions to be paid to police officers injured or killed while undertaking fire duties.

By 1893 it seems the vast majority of the purchases had been made and staff recruited and placed under the command of Chief Constable T.W. Byrne. On top of their police pay, recruits received an additional sum for firefighting duties. In 1894 the first true Worcester City Police Fire Brigade was formed at an annual cost of £89. In 1899 a decision was made that a Captain from the Norwich Union Fire

Office would attend all fires and in 1902, following a fiasco when nobody could turn on the high-pressure water supply, a 'turncock' from the Water Department was attached to the brigade. This arrangement would continue for the duration of the police brigade.

In 1862, the Norwich Union also opened a Fire Office in Kidderminster on the corner of Callows Lane and Church Street where an engine was available. In 1876 the Kidderminster Volunteer Fire Brigade was formed under the command of the Borough Architect Thomas Baker. This was quite a common arrangement. Later on the engine was moved from Callows Lane to its new base at the Town Hall.

Kidderminster is famous throughout the world for its carpets and there is no more famous carpet maker than Brintons, who in 1882 installed a whistle which would alert the crews if there was a fire. Many of the workers were volunteer firemen so when the whistle blasted once it signified a call in the 'town', two blasts, the 'foreign' (county) and three blasts Brintons itself! It became known as Brintons Bull.

The largest blaze for which the Borough of Kidderminster was required was the Watson Brothers Pike Mill, destroyed by a fire in 1886. Watson and Naylor built the Pike Mills in 1857 and it was a massive building, over 200ft by 70ft and 5 storeys high. On 1 July at approximately 11.15 p.m. an adjoining building appears to have been the site of the initial outbreak but nothing could prevent the fire spreading to the adjacent mill. The Watson and Naylor works brigade engine was stuck in the building and was also destroyed in the fire. Kidderminster, Norwich Union,

Worcester and Stourbridge, assisted by the works brigades of the other carpet factories, fought the blaze and struggled to bring it under control.

At 1 a.m. a gable end of the mill collapsed followed by the outer walls, sending shards of burning embers into the night sky. Several nearby carpet factories were in imminent danger of catching fire (G.W. Oldland and Company, Woodward Grovesnor and Company and Willis) and their workers were directed into fire parties to put out any flying burning embers. Part of the Willis factory did actually catch fire but it was put out before it posed a risk. The following morning the mill was a burnt out wreck and hundreds of people were out of work. The mills were demolished and it would take a further year to rebuild and get back to full production.

The Birmingham Fire Office, under the command of Mr Henry Burlingham, provided the means for firefighting in Evesham in the 1800s. They operated a rudimentary manual and other firefighting appliances.

In Willersey in 1843 a tragedy occurred which highlighted the danger of not having a fire engine available which could be on the scene quickly. A young mother, a housekeeper and five children were burned to death in a ferocious house fire. Broadway, the nearest town to Willersey, had no available fire engine and the building was totally destroyed by the time the Campden and Evesham brigades arrived. Broadway would not have its own manual for another fifty years!

Evesham Volunteer Fire Brigade was formed in 1895 under the command of a local man, Captain J. Huband. They operated out of the Town Hall buildings with

Memories! That's all the old station in Blockley is now. Having passed to North Cotswold County Council in 1931 it closed shortly after the end of nationalisation. All that is left to show it was a fire station is the three-phase electricity supply that powered the old call-in siren. You can just make out the size of the doors by the width of the lintel. Clive S. Shearman collection

Two views of the original Broadway Fire Station in Keytes Lane. The picture on the right shows the hose drying tower, for which planning permission was very difficult to obtain. The old station was demolished and is now the driveway for the new station. Worcester City and County Fire Brigade archive

a couple of bays opening directly onto Vine Street. This would be their base for the best part of seventy years. The strength of the brigade in these early days was a Captain, Lieutenant and ten firemen. They were supplied with a manual.

An entry found in *The Fireman* dated August 1896 states: 'The Evesham Fire Brigade will not attend fires in outlying parishes unless such parishes contribute to the maintenance of the brigade, but they will attend fires in such districts if asked to go by other brigades who may be in attendance and if they need further help.'

Some of the surrounding small parishes such as Beckford near Evesham operated a manual Shand Mason bought in 1865, which was an advanced machine for the period for such a small parish. Pebworth and Badsey were examples of brigades that relied solely on a hose cart.

A group in Honeybourne near Evesham decided in 1898 that fire provision was necessary and a hose and standpipe was costed. The local assurance companies declined to help so the council decided to pay £3 10s for the purchase and the equipment was stored in a cupboard in a local school. The Honeybourne Brigade's main aim was to provide an initial attack on the fire before the main brigade from Pershore arrived. Although Evesham is closer, the Borough in those days only provided cover to the town and unless annual rates were paid they did not attend.

Blockley Rural District Council purchased their first rudimentary manual in 1806 and in 1865 a Shand Mason manual engine was purchased through public subscription; this remained in operation until 1928. They had their base at Sheep Street in the village.

Broadway in the late 1800s had a very basic set-up with a standpipe and hose being kept at the premises of the local brazier, Chris Smith. At that time Broadway had mains water in the village and fireplugs had been built so a standpipe could be attached for firefighting purposes. After the Willersey fire in 1843 they were very

Broadway purchased a Merryweather & Sons Patent 'Four Poster' manual for use at their new Keytes Lane station. Clive S. Shearman collection

slow to act on the tragedy and following another disastrous fire at Lower Mill in 1897 the Broadway people had had enough and the Broadway Brigade was formed. Lower Mill was completely destroyed because it was out of reach of the mains, so the owners had to salvage what they could and stand and watch it burn to the ground. Action had to be taken and they approached Merryweathers and a Greenwich Manual was bought for the princely sum of £116 10s after a generous donation from a local man, Edgar Flower. This four-poster manual was similar to the machines the Metropolitan Fire Brigade was using in London.

The manual was built to be used by twenty-six men in teams of eight and two branchmen. The brigade now had their machine, the first Captain, Robert Cordell, was appointed and the station was built in Keytes Lane after land was donated by local man Issac Averill. They soon entered into agreements to provide cover for nearby Childswickham and Buckland Parish Councils.

Tenbury Volunteer Fire Brigade was formed in 1870 under the control of the parish council. This heralded the beginning of a unique association between the Hartland family and the brigade. On the formation of the brigade W. Hartland Snr became a fireman and then the engineer responsible for the manual hose cart and then the steamer. In 1907 his son William Hartland Jr joined the brigade after serving as a 'call boy' who was sent to alert everybody to a fire. He rose to become, like his father, the engineer responsible for making sure that the steamer was up to pressure and ready to fight a fire. They built up a high level of expertise as to when to drop the special 'Fusee' matches down the funnel of the boiler in order to light the pre-laid paper, wood and coal within the firebox. ('Fusee' matches were

The home of the Tenbury Wells Brigade was situated in Church Street. The late Reg Hartland collection

designed to burn and emit a great heat, in a strong wind, for a considerable period of time. It was estimated that the heat evolved was sufficient to boil a pint of water.)

William Hartland Jr would go on to serve fifty years and also to see his son Reginald Hartland join the local brigade, followed by a transfer to Worcester with Worcester City and County Fire Brigade. All in all, the family would serve the County of Worcestershire for an incredible 109 years.

Another firefighting weapon of the 1800s was the hose cart and most brigades operated one, including Tenbury Wells. Hose carts were manually pulled to the scene of a fire and the carts carried approximately ten lengths of rolled canvas hose, a standpipe for attaching the hose to the hydrant, a hydrant key and bar and a branch-pipe and nozzle. The effectiveness of the jet produced was entirely dependent upon the size of the nozzle used and the pressure and flow of water available within the water main. While such basic appliances may have been sufficient to provide meagre means of firefighting for a small community which had the benefit of a piped mains water supply to which hydrants were fitted, they were of no use whatsoever for remote and rural areas that were devoid of piped mains water. In many areas of rural Worcestershire this was largely the rule, rather than the exception. This was a situation which would prevail until the late 1950s.

An example of the shortcomings of the hose cart occurred when the Tenbury Wells Brigade attended a fire at Kyrewood Farm in 1914. Tenbury sent as first attendance the hose cart, but due to the farm being at the same height as the water source, insufficient pressure was produced so the steamer had to be sent for. After

The Tower Street Station in Old Town, Oldbury, was built in 1889 and opened in 1890. Dr Terry Daniels collection

arrival it was positioned by the pond and pumped water continuously for twelve hours. Due to the delay, the fire destroyed a large dutch barn containing 150 tons of hay. The cause of the fire was most likely children playing with matches.

Fire protection in the heavily industrial Borough of Oldbury in the 1800s had been the sole preserve of a number of works brigades, namely Ludwig Demuth (later Midland Tar Distillers), Chance and Hunt, Albright and Wilson and the Carriage Works, all of which had a manual appliance. The most serious fire to occur during this period of coverage happened during the spring of 1869 when an explosion caused a massive fire at the Demuth factory, which resulted in the deaths of four workers and partly destroyed the works. A later fire in 1879 in one of the pitch beds raised fears of another explosion. The local brigades were called for assistance and they included West Bromwich Volunteers and the works brigades of Tharis Cooper, Railway Carriage Company, Chance and Hunt and Chance Glass Works.

In 1887 the Local Board decided that Oldbury needed a brigade of its own and plans were drawn up by the local surveyor, Mr Harry Richardson CE, who would become its first Chief Officer. The plans included the selection and recruitment of the crew and the building of a station to house the appliance. A number of men gave their names as volunteers and the selection process was set in place. Once complete the brigade was formally organised at the beginning of 1889.

A new Shand Mason Steamer was purchased, rated at 350 gallons per minute (gpm), a fire escape and a multitude of firefighting kit. Unusually, two horses which were purchased outright! The site for the station was found and cleared of the old properties standing on it except for one which was retained as the engineer's house. The new station was opened in 1890 and Mr Richardson set about training his staff of two Lieutenants and twelve firemen with a real will.

A very early test for the fledgling Oldbury Brigade occurred on 17 April 1893 when a massive explosion rocked the Aluminium Works in Park Lane, Oldbury. A furnace used for the manufacture of sodium peroxide exploded, devastating the immediate area. It was a miracle nobody was killed and only two injured. Captain Richardson and his men were promptly on scene but there was very little to do but help in the evacuation and salvage work. The test had been passed and Oldbury no longer had to rely on the works brigades of the town.

Over the next few years the Oldbury Brigade consolidated its position with new equipment and an efficient callout system. This was also the start of an association with the Jeffries family, a local family which would provide members of the brigade until well into the next century. The dangers of the job were ever present, as seen in December 1893 when the brigade were called to assist the West Bromwich Brigade whose steamer had turned over going to a fire in the town, injuring a number of the crew.

The next major outbreak was not on their patch but in nearby Smethwick. On 2 February 1894 the Smethwick Volunteer Fire Brigade were tackling a fire at T. Bindley and Sons who produced glue, but it was well beyond their capability and reinforcements were drafted in from West Bromwich, Birmingham, Handsworth and the works brigades of Chances, Mitchells and Butlers, Tangye's and the Birmingham Wagon Works.

The largest fire in thirty years would see the Oldbury Brigade tested to the limits when a fire destroyed the main sawmill at the Carriage Works on 31 July 1900 at approximately 9 p.m. The brigade were now under the command of Captain Shipton who was on scene at 9.30 p.m. and quickly called for assistance from West Bromwich, Aston, Smethwick, Wolverhampton, Brierley Hill, Handsworth, Tipton, Wednesbury, Dudley Police and the works brigades of Chances, Cape Hill and Showells Brewery. The night sky was lit up as the flames exploded from the factory. The sawmill, which was full of valuable, highly flammable seasoned timber, was a total loss but the surrounding buildings and the thousands of tons of timber stacked outside were saved. The brigades pumped thousands of gallons of water onto the fire until the early hours of the following morning. The insurance estimate for the loss was put at £30,000, a fortune for the time.

On 16 September 1901 the brigade were called to a still fire at Demuth and Company. The fire was close to a group of gas tanks and the local people were evacuated as the tragedy of thirty-two years earlier was remembered. The brigade pumped for two hours to bring the fire under control but these were different times and Oldbury now had a highly efficient brigade capable of meeting most of the dangers thrown at them. During 1910 a sub-station was opened in the Warley district and was issued an Alldays and Onions motor tender. This supplemented the main station and reduced the need to call on outside assistance.

By 1878 the Bromsgrove Brigade was in a shambles. Many members were infirm, unfit and unprofessional. Action had to be taken, so the dilapidated St John Street

Captain Alderman and the men of the Bromsgrove Fire Brigade proudly assemble outside the Churchfields Fire Station with their Merryweather Greenwich Gem steamer c.1927. Bromsgrove Fire Station

base was closed and a number of members' services were dispensed with. The Bromsgrove Volunteers were formed and after a disastrous performance at a pumping competition at Stourbridge, the old Birmingham Fire Office manual was found to be obsolete. A new Merryweather No. 4 manual was purchased in 1879 and was stationed at the new Church Street headquarters. The Volunteers, under Lieutenant Hornsby, and later Captain John Humphreys, were now able to progress from good quality manual to a Merryweather Greenwich Gem steamer and then a motorised engine, and were once again pride of the town!

These were difficult and dangerous times with some small parishes paying subscriptions to other parishes so that their manual would turn out and provide cover, but if you were unable or unwilling to pay your building simply burnt to the ground. An entry in the *Berrows Journal* of October 1900 saw Bromsgrove Council hoping that neighbouring parishes would contribute towards the costs. Tardebigge and Upton Warren were undecided, but Stoke would not contribute and the Bromsgrove engine withdrew cover.

In 1881 Worcester City Council received a letter from the agents of the Lancashire Fire Insurance Company stating that they were withdrawing their manual engine. This was a national, not just local, decision based on the fact that they considered that local authorities were the proper custodians of their own fire protection. The Council was also informed that the Phoenix Fire Insurance

Company deemed Worcester so well protected by mains and hydrants that they were sending their manual to Droitwich to provide protection there. However, the Norwich Union Insurance Company decided that they were staying and that they were going to buy the latest Merryweather steamer to supplement the old manual *Niagara*. The Council was not very happy about the loss of fire cover. It was correct that Worcester was providing new water mains all over the city but nobody knew how efficient they were. A test would have to take place.

On 28 April 1881 the Norwich Union Fire Insurance Fire Brigade, under the command of Captain Sayce, were requested to bring the new steam engine to London Road, Worcester, to take part in the test. A large crowd had gathered including Mr Hill MP and some members of the Town Council to witness a demonstration of the new corporation water main and see if the pressure was sufficient to provide water for the engine. The district manager of the Norwich Union Fire Office, former Captain A.P. Watkins, was in charge of the test. The steamer was quickly fired up and after a series of tests the main was found to provide only sufficient water for four-minute bursts before replenishment, as the steamer was throwing out upwards of 360 gallons a minute, a colossal improvement on what the old manuals could generate. The Worcester City Police Fire Brigade, who were in attendance with their manual and hose, connected a hose to the main but found the pressure only provided a feeble jet. The net result of the test was that due to their loyalty to the city, the Norwich Union Fire Insurance Company were given all the Council's insurance for fire protection and provision.

In December 1882 the brigade were called to a large fire at Stanford Court, a large mansion on the outskirts of Worcester. Under Captain Sayce the men were kept engaged for three days and nights in appalling conditions before the fire was finally subdued. They had to contend with heavy snow, frozen hosepipes, fatigue and then a very cold, wet drive back to Worcester when it was all over.

The Norwich Union Fire Brigade provided cover not only for the city but also the surrounding district, as entries for 1882 in *The Fireman* testify. Under the command of either Captain Sayce or his deputy, Captain Gibbs, the steamer attended hayrick fires at Cummins Farm, Hindlip. Hindlip Hall owned their own manual which was providing an initial attack on the fire. Further fires occurred at Cotheridge, Pitmaston, St Johns and again Cotheridge where it transpired that a local boy, whose parent was employed on the farm, had been playing with matches and had deliberately started the fire.

During 1894 Worcester City Council built a high-level reservoir in the Rainbow Hill area which provided excellent water and hydrant pressure in that part of the city and its surrounds. The Worcester Police Fire Brigade, who were still using a hose cart and standpipe connected to a hydrant, complained that water pressure in other areas was still poor, especially in the vicinity of the cathedral.

Typical of the type of provision for protection against fire was the arrangement Newnham Bridge had in that they paid Tenbury Wells RDC a token £2 per month to provide cover for their area. Another of these agreements was in force in Redditch where the engines protected the Alvechurch and Beoley parishes in Bromsgrove RDC and the Studley parish in Alcester RDC.

Following Captain Harper's retirement, the Birmingham Fire Office in Malvern was run by Captain J. Hamsher who would serve the brigade for seventeen years until he resigned in 1887. He was succeeded in 1890 by George McCan. He, along

Above: *Captain Thorpe and the men of the Malvern Wells Fire Brigade in the doorway of their new Station c.1900. The sign in the background reads 'Ready and Willing'.* Malvern Museum

Opposite above: *A fine shot of William Thorpe and the men of the Malvern Fire Brigade. c.1900.* Malvern Museum collection

Opposite below: *The successful bidder was Shand Mason & Co. who contracted the work out to a Manchester firm, William Rose & Co. They delivered the steamer to Malvern in 1897.* Ron Henderson collection

with thirteen firemen, would serve the town out of their Victoria Road base until the arrival of William O. Thorpe in 1909. George McCan's trusty and long-serving Lieutenant was H. Keen who ultimately became one of the first firemen in Worcestershire to lay down his life in the line of duty. An entry found in *The Fireman* dated August 1896 states:

> The parishes of Guarlford and Newland have agreed to contribute to the expenses of the Malvern Fire Brigade, on condition that they will be entitled to the services of the brigade in the event of a fire.

One of the largest fires attended by the Malvern Brigade was in June 1896 when the Imperial Hotel, Great Malvern caught fire. The local brigade called for the attendance of the Norwich Union Fire Brigade from Worcester as the fire was starting to get away from them. Captain Sayce sent one of his men ahead on a steam train to get an idea of what faced them as they made their way on the steamer drawn by four horses. The steamer was put to work immediately and once a good water supply was attained the fire was subdued. The damage caused by the fire was estimated at £5,000. During October of the same year the same two brigades fought a fire at Severn End, the seat of the Lechmere family. The fire broke out in the early morning and due to the lack of telegraph a messenger was sent by bicycle to Worcester nine miles distant to summon help. They received the call at 6 a.m. and had arrived and got water onto the fire at 7 a.m., a great achievement. Unfortunately, the fire had taken a firm hold and large parts of the historic Tudor house were destroyed. This fire was the catalyst for the Malvern Brigade to convert to a steam-powered pump and tenders were sought from various firms.

The second station built in Malvern was at the Council Yard in Grundys Lane, Malvern Wells. Built in 1897, the first Lieutenant was D. Jones in 1880. Lieutenant Vernall succeeded him in 1885 and along with a number of firemen they operated a Plan D Merryweather manual with a built-in hose box.

The Malvern Wells Brigade would use the Merryweather manual well into the next century along with a hose cart and self-propelled fire escape. The station would also be summoned by messenger and unless he was on horseback it would be a very slow and arduous task.

In Stourbridge in the 1870s fire protection was provided by the Phoenix Insurance Company and the Alliance Insurance Company, who both had manuals. They were very reliant on messengers summoning the engines, which were garaged at various locations in the town. The most memorable fire of note was on 13 October 1877 when due to a number of factors Stourton Court, the home of local dignitary Captain Foster, burnt to the ground. This fire was a watershed in the history of firefighting in Stourbridge. In 1879 a local dignitary, Henry Turney, decided to form the Stourbridge Volunteer Fire Brigade and the Stourbridge Commissioners transferred an old Alliance manual to the brigade to use at the new Market Street station.

The brigade were initially composed of Captain Turney, two Lieutenants and twelve firemen. To go with the manual, the brigade were also issued with a fire escape from the Royal Society of the Protection of Life from Fire. Captain Turney would go on to mould the Stourbridge Brigade into a highly professional team and this would epitomise his tenure. His energy was infectious and on the arrival of the

The Merryweather manual of the Borough of Bewdley Fire Brigade c.1910 outside the Guildhall,
which served as the base for the engine for a further half a century. The late Reg Hartland collection

new Merryweather steamer purchased through public subscription in 1880, the brigade became one of the most efficient in the region. In 1884 the fire station was connected to the firemen's houses via electric bells and this speeded up attendance times and made the messenger system virtually redundant. In 1888 the new station was built at the old Corn Exchange in New Street and the brigade strength was the Captain, Lieutenant, Superintendent, Hon. Surgeon and sixteen firemen. The appliances comprised the steamer, manual, hose cart, one escape, 1,800ft hose, two ambulances and scaling ladders.

The Captain found himself in an enviable position, but this success had come at the expense of his health. He should have taken it easier but not Captain Turney, he became the driving force and one of the founders of the fledgling Fire Brigades Union, ultimately becoming its Honorary Secretary. His bad health finally caught up with him and he was forced to resign in 1890. He retired to Gorleston, near Great Yarmouth where in 1892 after a bout of influenza he died peacefully. He was succeeded by Captain Connor Walker, who took a contingent of the Stourbridge Brigade down to Norfolk for the funeral. He took over the legacy of Captain Turney and took the brigade forward into the new century.

The Borough of Bewdley had a fire presence as early as 1709 when it was recorded that an engine was kept in a church in the town. This manual was bought towards the end of the 1890s and would serve well into the 1930s when a Bedford motor pump would replace it. It was kept at the Guildhall under the control of the foreman, Harry Evans.

Another massive blaze towards the end of the century happened at the Thomas White Timber Yard in New Road, Kidderminster on 13 August 1896. At midnight a strong wind was blowing and a fire quickly whipped up and spread like wildfire. The new Pike Mills Factory Brigade fought the blaze along with Kidderminster, Stourbridge and Norwich Union Fire Brigades. The fire was massive and was visible from as far away as Cutnall Green. On the following morning the brigades were starting to win the battle but it would take the rest of the day to finally subdue the flames. A shed across the road in Oxford Street was said to house a consignment of two tons of matches, which would have razed the area to the ground if it had caught fire.

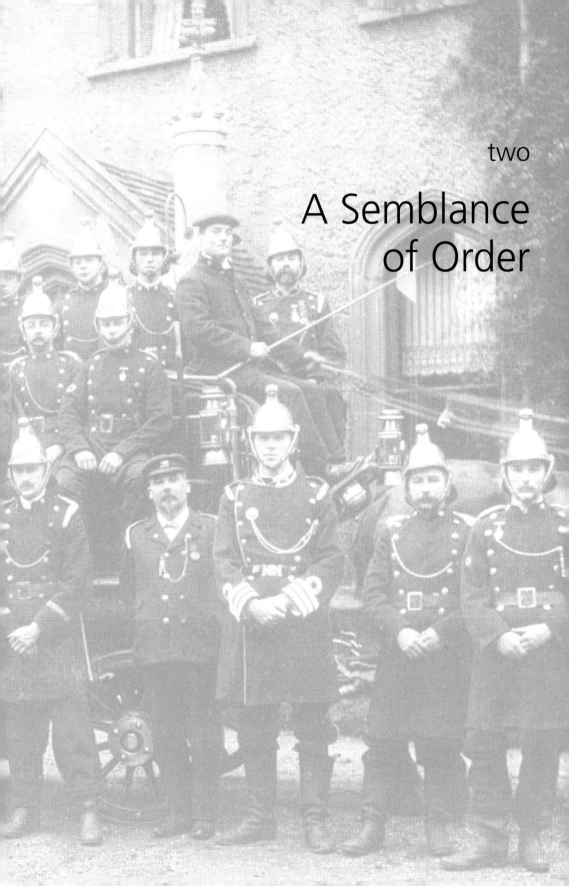

two

A Semblance
of Order

Worcestershire at the beginning of the 1890s was seeing the advent of steam-powered pumps taking over from the manuals, though still pulled by horses. Kidderminster, Pershore, Redditch and Tenbury Wells would purchase fine examples of the latest Shand Mason model. Bromsgrove, Stourbridge and the Norwich Union, Worcester would go for Merryweathers.

Once fired, the Shand Mason steamer could produce up to 120lb pressure in approximately seven minutes and was then able to pump water at its design specification of up to 300 gallons per minute. For the earlier manuals it took twenty-six men to produce the 115 gallons per minute rate required. When you think of all the volunteers that were required for the old manuals you can see firefighting had taken a quantum leap forward. Also the beer bill disappeared virtually overnight!

The men of the Kidderminster Brigade pose with their new Shand Mason Steamer c.1900. D. Oliver collection

Captain John Kendrick and the men of the Redditch Volunteer Fire Brigade show how firefighting has progressed from the single jet of the manual to the multi-jets that the new Shand Mason steamer could produce once it was up to steam. The engine turned out to be a great crowd-pleaser! Bob Morris collection

Money was still short and hard to come by for some areas so other ways had to be found to purchase the new technology. Some equipment was bought out of public subscription such as at Pershore, where in 1900 a Shand Mason was bought to operate from the Bridge Street base; the steamer remained in operation until 1933.

Pershore Fire Brigade was typical of the type of rural brigade around at the turn of the century. The main shortcoming was lack of experience, with some brigades not having a single call in a year. The good leaders were not short on motivation and arranged training evenings which would turn into what we now refer to as

Right: *Lieutenant Field stands with the new Shand Mason steamer delivered to the Pershore Fire Brigade in 1900.* Marshall Wilson collection

Below: *Pershore 'callout': They were on a shout, but with the novelty of early photography they could not resist stopping and saving the moment! The fire station is visible in the background.* Bernard Poultney collection

'drill nights'. At these get-togethers basic firefighting techniques were taught and the men were shown how to maintain the equipment, which quickly deteriorated if not looked after properly. Also, people were allocated certain tasks at a callout – one of the main ones being to catch and collect the horses. No horses, no turnout (or a very long pull!).

In many districts the water undertakers insisted that water for firefighting should not be taken from hydrants attached to their mains, unless their representative (the turncock) was present. Often, on hearing the alarm, the turncock immediately reported to the fire station and rode on the appliance with the crew. Turncocks took no part in active firefighting and were not kitted out in a fireman's uniform, but were often distinctive by their company's uniform. A turncock may be identified standing behind the trailer pump in the photograph on page 63 depicting the Droitwich Brigade. The turncock played a very important role during the days when a fire was attacked with a jet of water via a line of hose, which was obtained directly from a hydrant on the mains supply. If the pressure and flow of the water main proved to be inadequate, the turncock, having the knowledge of the local mains network, was able to manipulate the appropriate valves of adjacent mains in an attempt to divert and improve the supply as necessary.

Upon the death of Captain Turney the Stourbridge Volunteers came under the command of Captain Connor Walker, a local solicitor who on being offered the job initially declined until he had become versed in the art of firefighting among the ranks. He eventually accepted the job and served with distinction from 1893 until his death in 1901. During his tenure the parishes of Wollaston and Upper Swinford were added to the fire cover provided by the Volunteers.

The new Captain J. Donaldson Harward assumed command and this was well received as he had risen from the ranks. In 1902, partly through subscription and partly through good housekeeping, a new Merryweather steamer was delivered at a cost of £496. The brigade were now at their most efficient and were answering on average about a dozen fires a year. Not many, you may think, but they were drilling every week for two hours. On 12 February 1903 the new steamer averted a near disaster at the premises of Edward Webbs Flour Mill at Wordsley. This was the third major fire at the mills since 1883, when the building was nearly destroyed. The mill was a massive three-storey structure built in 1849 and was one of the major risks in Wordsley. On discovering the fire at 3 a.m. messengers were sent to summon the nearest brigade, which were Stourbridge Volunteers under the command of Lieutenant Ford, who responded at 3.52 a.m. They arrived at 4.10 a.m. and set to work with their steamer and manual from a nearby canal. The Brierley Hill Volunteers, under the command of Lieutenant Beckley, arrived shortly afterwards and set into a nearby well with their steamer. Shortly afterwards there was an explosion, probably of dust, and the fire burst through the roof and from this point the building was lost and the job became one of containment. The brigades prevented the fire reaching a valuable seed warehouse and they were congratulated on this fact.

Another major Stourbridge fire of the period was the disastrous outbreak at Enville Hall, the residence of the Countess of Stamford and Warrington on 25 November 1904. Luckily the household had a Tilley and Company manual and hose and members quickly set about tackling the fire, which was confined initially to a bedroom. Realising the fire was getting away from them, messengers were sent

Above: *In 1901 H. Hemming, the landlord of the Mason Arms public house (seen on the right of the picture), organized the Pebworth village Volunteer Fire Brigade. This comprised a team of local men including a turncock (pictured third from the right) equipped with a hose cart that was manufactured by the village wheelwright. The fire station was established in a section of barn at Baldwins Farm, Dorsington Road. The volunteers were summoned by tolling the No.5 bell at the nearby parish church. Each volunteer was issued with a simple rulebook – the rules were few, simple, yet very exacting. Regular training and drills was the order of the day.*

Above left: *The name fades and* (left) *Captain H. Hemming and his men on the same patch of ground over a century ago.* Clive S. Shearman collection and Crighton Cotton collection

The men of the Stourbridge Volunteer Fire Brigade with the newly delivered Merryweather steamer in 1902. It would quickly be put to the test at the disastrous Enville Hall fire. Stourbridge Library

to summon the Stourbridge Volunteers. The Volunteers responded initially with Lieutenant Walker and the manual closely followed, once it was hitched to four horses, by the steamer under the command of Lieutenant Stanley. Due to snow lying on the roads the journey was slow and very hazardous with the brigade finally arriving at 3.40 a.m., a full hour after being alerted.

Both machines quickly set into the nearby lake and started to throw jets onto the burning property. Stourbridge Volunteers had also alerted extra men to bring the reserve steamer to the scene and, pulled by a team of three horses, she arrived at 5 a.m. and was put to work. Captain Harward arrived to take charge of the firefighting. Exhaustion is always a problem at large fires and there were no reliefs in those days so you just had to 'grin and bear it'. By 11 a.m. the fight was starting to be won and columns of white smoke replaced the flames. After twenty-four hours of sheer exhaustion and courage the fire was surrounded but it continued to burn on and off for a couple of days and smoulder for a further two weeks. The building was a shell but the valuable silver and the paintings and books had been saved. The Volunteers had bought the time that was needed to do this but it had come at a cost of three of their number injured. One amusing story from the incident was that due to the freezing weather the firemen were quickly wet through. The generous 'gentlemen' householders threw their wardrobes open for the firemen to get dried out and they must have looked the smartest attired firemen ever to fight a blaze!

These were not the only injuries received by the brigade as on 1 January 1907 the Volunteers were called to an outbreak at G.K.Harrisons Ltd in Brettell Lane in the town. The crews got the manual away and the steamer hitched and that also proceeded to the fire, but unbeknown to the crew the lead horse was not secured and bolted from the engine, pulling the driver off his seat. Fireman Foster was knocked unconscious but later recovered from his injuries.

Stourbridge had enlarged its sphere of influence as a result of having two engines, attending fires as far afield as Kinver, Wombourne, Alveley and four miles from Bridgnorth. Bridgnorth did possess its own engine but having only one it was constrained to stay in the town.

Under Captain Sayce the Norwich Union Fire Service was becoming known nationally. He was a far-sighted man who could see that the days of horsepower were drawing to a close. During 1901 he decided, with the agreement of the Norwich Union, to have the 1881 Merryweather steamer converted into a self-propelling engine. Mr C.T. Crowden of Leamington Spa was commissioned to do the work under the supervision of Captain Sayce and the engine was delivered back a few weeks later after having its boiler adapted to power the road wheels as well as the pump.

As is usually the case, one incident always makes the press. In Blackstones book, *A History of the British Fire Service*, the local brigade were portrayed as laughing

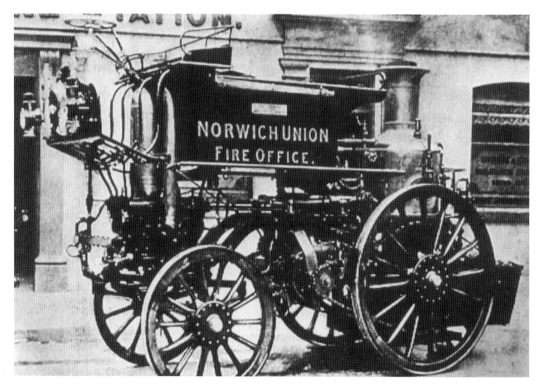

The early Merryweather steamer outside the Angel Place Station in 1901 after conversion. Aviva Plc archive

stocks due to the conversion of the above machine. *Berrows Journal* of 1901 records that 'On its first call it made very prompt time to a fire in Kempsey'. Unfortunately along the way it was causing mayhem, with numerous fires caused by sparks from the fire due to the lack of a spark protector (a mesh bubble on the top of the stack). The old manual following behind put out the fires as it too was going to the outbreak. The conversion showed up many shortcomings but the idea was sound. It was the first motorised appliance in the country to get to a fire under its own propulsion and provided the inspiration for the 'Fire King' range of appliances.

In 1905 the local office of the Norwich Union Insurance Company in Angel Place, Worcester purchased a Merryweather Fire King self-propelled 400Gpm steam pump, named *Scarlet Pimpernel* and registered FK201, for their Five Ways office. For the time this was state-of-the-art firefighting and it was demonstrated to local dignitaries at every opportunity.

Considerable interest was aroused on 28 July 1905 in Ledbury, Herefordshire with the visit of Captain Sayce and the new Merryweather Fire King. This was the engine's first journey out of the 'Faithful City' and was considered to be a real test of its performance. It journeyed via Malvern over the British Camp pass and down into Ledbury. On arrival Captain Hopkins and a considerable crowd of local townsfolk inspected the engine. If called out in an emergency it could traverse the distance at 20mph, in approximately one hour after being gotten up to steam.

The Merryweather Fire King on its delivery to Worcester in 1905. Captain Sayce is seen behind the wheel on one of its numerous test runs. Don Oliver collection

Above: *Captain Alfred Sayce (wearing a cap) is seen standing on the Merryweather Fire King* Scarlet Pimpernel *on Flower Day 1916. His son Alfred William Sayce is sitting next to him.* Berrows Newspapers archive

NORWICH UNION FIRE INSURANCE SOCIETY, LTD.

FOUNDED 1797.

ACCIDENT.

LOWEST
RATES
OF
PREMIUM.

FIRE.

WORKMEN'S
COMPENSATION.

PROMPT AND
LIBERAL
SETTLEMENT
OF LOSSES.

MARINE.

Risks inspected and Quotations given on application for all classes of Insurance.

District Managers : Messrs. WATKINS & SAYCE,
Telephone No. 10.   Angel Place, WORCESTER.

The Norwich Union is the only office in Worcester maintaining a Fire Brigade.
No charge is made for the services of the Brigade when the Property is insured in this Office.

XIX.

Upton-upon-Severn Volunteers had been used to pulling a hose cart for the better part of the last century, but things were about to change. This volunteer force was in the charge of a local buisnessman, Captain Fred Soars. The appliance which would bring a change to the very exerting challenge of hauling a hose cart was a horse-drawn manual. Originally delivered in 1857 to the Norwich Union Insurance Company in Worcester, the old manual engine *Niagara* had given good service, but

Upton-upon-Severn Volunteers c.1906 with the manual donated by the Norwich Union Insurance Co.
Upton-upon-Severn Museum

in 1906 it was deemed surplus to requirements after the delivery of the
Merryweather Fire King, and was kindly donated to the Upton-upon-Severn
Volunteer FB to augment their hose cart. It was kept at their station in New Street
and it operated until 1929. Incredibly good value!

On 19 September 1906 the Malvern and Malvern Wells appliances were called to
a massive outbreak on the North Hill, Malvern. The fire could be seen over most of
Worcestershire and taxed the small brigades to their limits.

The Stourport-on-Severn UDC were another brigade who used a manual and
then a steamer well into the 1930s. The volunteer crew were alerted to the fact
there was a fire call by the bullhorn of local firm Holbrooks. It would be one of
their machines, along with appliances from Kidderminster and Stourbridge
Boroughs and the local works brigades, that fought the Brintons Carpet Factory fire
on 23 January 1907 which destroyed large parts of the factory and cost £20,000, a
huge amount for the time. An amazing fact has come to light about this fire.
Despite the lead horse dropping dead at Overley and the crew having to drag it to
the side of the road and then assisted the remaining horse, the Stourbridge crew still
managed to arrive first on the scene – quite a feat of professionalism!

On 20 July 1906 the Redditch steamer and manual under the command of
Captain Perrins attended an outbreak at the Beoley Mills which resulted in the
destruction of large parts of the premises and cost approximately £2,000. In 1908
the Bromsgrove steamer and manual, under the command of Captain Leadbetter,
were called to an outbreak at the Victor Drury Boot Factory. This was a massive
factory which employed hundreds of local people. The fire quickly got away from

Above and right:
*Captain Hughes and
the men of the
Borough of
Kidderminster Fire
Brigade on AB4404,
their 45hp Napier
motor tender.* Don
Oliver and
C. Wooldridge

the crews, which led to the roof being lost and parts of the exterior wall collapsing
into the street.

Firefighting technology in Worcestershire had moved on with the arrival of the
steam-driven pumps. These steamers in the large towns were what the 'Dennis
Sabre' is today. The best equipment was stationed where the biggest risk to life
existed, but what the brigades of the time did not have was the ability to quickly

The aftermath of the Brintons Carpet fire on the morning of 24 January 1907. The roof has collapsed, taking the floors down into the basement. The building was a total loss. C. Wooldridge collection

call on reinforcements of additional appliances. The days where more appliances were only a radio call away was another fifty years off! If a large fire got away from the initial attendance the building was normally lost and attention would be switched to containment and protection of neighbouring property.

Many local stately homes and large institutions had fire provision. It varied from a few buckets, fire hooks and hose to a complete machine. Obviously cost played a great part in what could be afforded, but the most audacious purchase must have been made by the local lunatic asylum at Powick near Worcester. The average Victorian lunatic asylum was a massive imposing stone structure, and if a fire caught hold and got into the roof it would be well beyond the capability of most fire brigades of the period. They were also very high life risks, especially if a fire took hold at night, so all in all, they posed considerable problems for local authorities.

The Worcester County and City Asylum at Powick was like most of its contempories, built just outside the city it served. Towards the end of the 1890s the water pressure was starting to cause the management serious concerns should a fire occur. In 1908 the well-known fire engine makers Merryweather and Sons were consulted and recommended a static steam pump as the solution to their problems. A 'Greenwich Gem' steam pump of 400Gpm was ordered and installed along with fire-main piping and hydrants and ancillary firefighting equipment. Once fired, the boiler could be got up to steam in six minutes, providing water to the hose at

A Merryweather advert of 1907 showing the newly delivered 'Fixed Gem' steam fire pump for Powick Asylum.

Droitwich Borough and Rural District Councils Fire Brigade pose with their Shand Mason manual at the back of the Friar Street Station c.1900. Droitwich Fire Brigade chose leather as opposed to brass for their helmets. This view of the rear yard shows the station before the watchroom was added and the steel ladder reversed. J.O. Brettell collection

various points throughout the hospital. A thorough test of the system occurred on 17 June 1908 with all the officials being thoroughly impressed with the results. Powick Asylum finally had protection; some others were not quite so lucky, experiencing fires which claimed the lives of many patients.

Droitwich Borough built their fire station in Friar Street during 1892. Equipment at that time comprised a hose cart that also carried a jumping sheet and a horse-drawn manual, which had been donated by the Phoenix Fire Insurance Company. A wheeled escape was stationed in the market arcade beneath the Town Hall. The firemen, who were paid a retaining fee of £3 per annum and half a crown for each turnout, were summoned by the gas works steam whistle being blasted continuously for three minutes. During 1897 the council purchased a second-hand steamer from Merryweather at a cost of £150.

In 1901 the boiler of the steamer became defective and lengthy correspondence ensued between the Town Clerk and Merryweather. Coltman and Sons eventually refurbished the boiler, at a cost of £80. During that year additional problems arose as George Bourne reported that he was unable to continue to supply horses for Fire Brigade use. Much to the dismay of the Council at the proposed high cost, Mr Meads offered to supply horses as the need arose, at £5 a time. The steamer was used at the time of the most notable fire of the period, when the Droitwich Town Mills caught fire on 22 August 1909. Assistance was also obtained from Bromsgrove Fire Brigade, who responded with their steamer.

Above and below: *The day after the night before: the burnt out remains of W. Norton, Rollermillar & Corn Merchants, known as the 'Town Mills', shows the extent of the previous night's conflagration.* J.O. Brettell collection

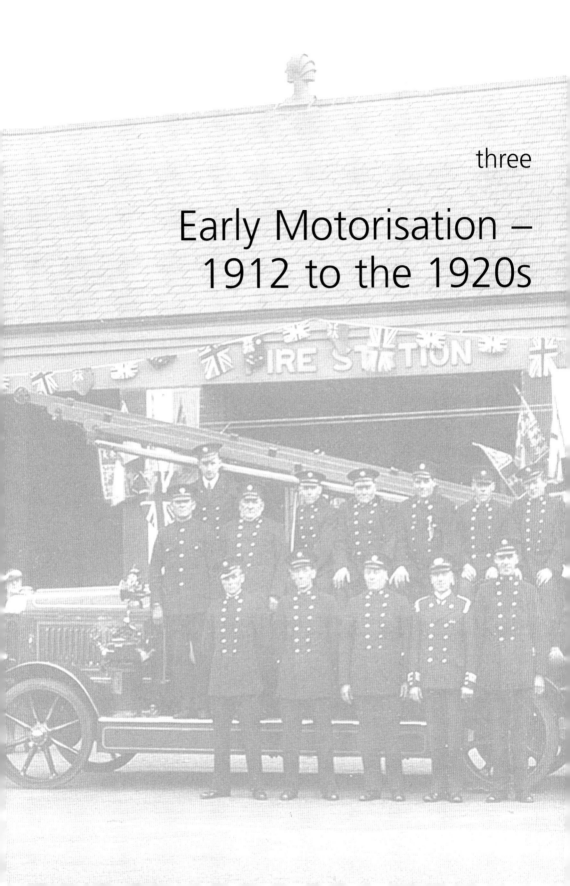

three

Early Motorisation –
1912 to the 1920s

The arrival of the combustion engine was to revolutionise the firefighting appliance. The horse was made redundant virtually overnight, and names such as Leyland, Dennis and Albion would become familiar sights on the road.

Early petrol-driven appliances operated as two basic types. The machine had a pump driven from the road engine via a power take off from the gearbox; the appliance usually carried a 30 or 35ft extension ladder. The pump escape was similar, but carried a wheeled escape ladder.

The bodywork of both types of appliance followed the same basic pattern as those designed and used for horse-drawn appliances, which was the brainchild of James Earl Braidwood, the former Chief Officer of the London Fire Brigade. The Braidwood body, as it was familiarly known, was essentially a box with hinged side doors to carry hose and associated equipment, with footboards running the length of the vehicle on which the firemen could stand and ride.

Malvern Town purchased a ground-breaking Dennis N Series chemical escape in 1912. The 'Chemical Engine' was, in effect, a large scale soda/acid fire extinguisher, to which a 120ft length of 1-inch bore reinforced rubber hose, complete with shut-off nozzle, was permanently connected. The hose was coiled on a revolving drum, mounted on the top of the fire engine. The water storage comprised a large enclosed copper cylinder of approximately forty gallons capacity, to which a measured quantity of bicarbonate of soda was added. A large, measured, sealed phial of sulphuric acid was held within a sealed cage within the body of the cylinder; by the operation of a lever or handle the sealed phial could easily be ruptured and the mixing of the two chemicals in solution resulted in the rapid production of carbonic acid gas which pressurised the vessel to approximately 100lbs per square inch and expelled the water through the hose. Very effective for the time!

On 10 August 1912, Chief Officer Thorpe of the Malvern Brigade was on a Fire Brigades Union camp at Crystal Palace in London along with 1,100 other firemen and their array of manuals, steamers and motorised engines. The highlight of the event would be a review by the specially invited guest, HRH King Manuel of Portugal. The Dennis was ground-breaking technology of the time and the Malvern combination was singled out for special attention by the King. A special honour awaited the Malvern crew as Lord Londesborough, who at the time was President of the FBU, stopped the Dennis as it was passing the royal stand and the King stepped forward, broke a bottle of wine over the turbine pump and christened her *Lady Grey*.

When the *Lady Grey* was ready to be delivered to Malvern from Dennis Brothers in Guildford, Surrey, Chief Officer Thorpe went down to accept her and bring her

Dennis Brothers N Series Chemical Escape Lady Grey *of the Malvern Fire Brigade c.1912 showing the soda acid tank.* Transbus Dennis International Ltd

back. This might not seem much today, when you can get into a fully air-conditioned cab and zip down the motorway and be back home in a couple of hours, but in those days it was a two-day run and if the weather was bad it was a really cold and unpleasant duty. The Dennis representative, Mr Hindson, drove the machine back, leaving Guildford on the Sunday at 10.50 a.m. and arriving at Oxford at 1.50 p.m. On leaving Oxford they came across the Cotswolds, arriving at Cheltenham at 5.10 p.m. At 6.10 p.m. they left Cheltenham and arrived in Malvern via Tewkesbury at 7.15 p.m., to be met by a large crowd. The journey had taken over six hours at an average speed of 22mph. That was really good going for the day and the 'Lady' had performed beautifully, never missing a beat!

The final story regarding the *Lady Grey* is a rather sad one. The Coroner Mr G.F.S. Brown opened an inquest on 22 August 1916 at Malvern Hospital into the death of the popular Lieutenant H. Keen.

He heard from a number of witnesses about the tragic events of an ordinary farm fire at Blackmore Park near Hanley Swan the previous Thursday. The brigade were dispatched on the *Lady Grey* from Victoria Road with Chief Officer Thorpe OIC (Officer in Charge) and the deceased as SIC (Second in Charge) and a full crew. They arrived at 6.30 a.m. to find a hayrick burning fiercely out of control. The crew immediately set to work fighting the fire. At approximately 9.30 a.m. the chief decided to send some of the men back to Malvern as the steamer had now arrived and would stay until the fire was completely out.

They returned to the *Lady Grey*, which had been pumping now continuously for three hours on a mixture of paraffin and petrol, only to accidentally flood the carburettor. The deceased checked and saw all the ignitions were switched off. To restart these old engines somebody had to turn the starting handle once for each of the four cylinders to get them charged. The driver would then have to switch on the accumulator to start the engine. On this occasion it would not fire. A number of firemen went through this process until Lieutenant Keen was operating the starting handle and Fireman Lucas was in the driver's seat. Fireman Lucas could remember the deceased turning the starting handle and standing up, but as he went to fire the engine the deceased went out of his view, the engine fired and started to run as normal. As Fireman Lucas looked up he was horrified to see the deceased lying on his back with his face covered in blood. Attempts at first aid were futile and the deceased was taken to Malvern Hospital but he never regained consciousness and was pronounced dead. The investigation showed that the mixture of fuel and the repeated attempts at starting the engine had resulted in a 'back-fire' which had turned the starting handle violently, catching the deceased fully in the face. He was more than likely unconscious before he hit the ground and the force of this had fractured his skull. Lieutenant Keen had served the brigade for thirty-five years and was greatly respected. He was afforded a full service funeral.

The Stourbridge Volunteer Fire Brigade has always been in the forefront of technology and they did not disappoint when they paid £1,400 for their first motorised appliance, a Dennis N chassis with Braidwood-bodied pump, in 1916. The new Captain C.S. Trow and Lieutenant T.L. Walker were proud to be present when the engine was christened *Douglas* after the previous Captain E.D. Trow who had been influential in raising the money. The Dennis was rated at 700Gpm and carried forty gallons of water in a tank. 1,600ft of hose was stored in lockers and the main rescue ladder was a 35ft Bailey ladder.

The proud Stourbridge Volunteer Brigade pose with their brand new Dennis N Series pump Douglas *outside the Smithfield Station, c.1916.* Stourbridge Library

The first major fire was at Prestwood Hall on 22 January 1922. Prestwood Hall at Stewponey on the banks of the River Stour had for many years been the residence of the Foley family, but had recently been purchased with the purpose of converting it into offices for the Staffordshire and Wolverhampton and Dudley Hospitals for the treatment of tuberculosis. The fire was first spotted at 12.30 p.m. by a local man who thought that somebody was on the premises but later, when the smoke issuing was more than normal, the building was checked and a fire was found. The Stourbridge Volunteers were alerted at 3.37 p.m. and the force turned out with the first aid pump and the Dennis. They were on the scene within twenty minutes and pumping from both hydrant and open water. The resources of the Brierley Hill, Wolverhampton and Dudley Brigades were requested for additional assistance but the building was already lost and the priority now became the salvage and containment of the fire. This would not be achieved until well into the following day and the final bill for the fire was in excess of £20,000.

To give you an idea of what a small brigade cost to run, the *Fire Journal* of 1920 detailed a number of brigades across the country, including Malvern UDC, and looked at what they had done in 1919. Malvern UDC total expenditure was £501; they attended twelve calls of which eight were fires; their largest risk was the Morgan Car Company works but there were many hotels and boarding houses that posed a large life risk; and the total fire loss for that year was £2,200. I suspect this was pretty typical for Worcestershire.

In 1919 the Oldbury Brigade was aware that the steamer was getting quite antiquated and was due for replacement. It had given good service over the years as the brigade got busier but the days of horse and steamer in conjunction were drawing to a close. Different companies were to tender, with Leyland and Company of Chorley, Lancashire being the successful bidder. A Leyland FE1 pump escape AB7432 was delivered to the main station in 1920 (registered on 6 December 1919). Its first major fire would be at the Worcestershire Maltings Ltd premises in Langley when one of the large buildings caught fire on 26 September 1925. Assistance was requested and the Smethwick Volunteers and the nearby Showells Brewery Brigade came and after twelve hours of pumping using a number of jets the fire was surrounded.

In 1919 Bromsgrove UDC purchased AB6647, a Leyland FE1 appliance to replace the steamer at their Churchfields station. This was more than likely a second-hand chassis from the War Department. After the end of the First World War Leyland and Company had purchased back hundreds of lorries and stripped them down to their chassis. The chassis were reconditioned and then converted into whatever type of vehicle was required. They provided a much-needed stop-gap chassis until full production was resumed after the war.

A real blow occurred shortly afterwards as Chief Leadbetter of the Bromsgrove Fire Brigade retired in September 1920 due to ill health but was granted the rank of Honorary Chief Officer. He had been an excellent servant to the town and would be sorely missed.

During 1920 a 30hp Panhard motorised tender AB6838 was delivered to the Lye and Wollescote UDC Brigade.

On 10 January 1920 a fire occurred at Thomasson and Company in Shrub Hill, Worcester. A japanning shed was destroyed but the Norwich Union, Worcester City Police and Heenan Froude Brigades who fought the blaze saved the rest of the

The Leyland FE1 Pump Escape delivered to Oldbury Brigade in 1920 on the occasion of the Coronation in 1935. Dr Terry Daniels

Civic dignitaries and the crew stand outside the station on the occasion of the Coronation in 1935. Dr Terry Daniels

The Bromsgrove crew during a procession with the reconditioned Leyland FE1 pump. Note the spoked wheels and solid rubber tyres which were a feature of the time. The late Reg Hartland collection

factory. A massive fire occurred in Worcester during 1920 at the premises of the Worcester Ice Factory on the Bromyard Road. The factory stored massive amounts of bacon for national consumption and was severely damaged in the blaze with costs put in excess of £4,000. The Norwich Union, Worcester City Police and Cadbury Brothers Ltd with their Merryweather steamer fought the blaze. Reports in *The Fireman* journal show that during the 1920s the lack of a motorised appliance and an up-to-date station in Worcester were a local scandal.

During 1920 an inquest was opened into the death of a ten year old boy who was killed while riding to a fire on Blockley's horse-drawn Shand Mason manual. The child had known all the firemen well, especially fireman Keen who was the driver that day. On seeing that the crew was short that day he mounted the engine and took his seat. When one of the horses bolted another member of the crew told him to jump but for some reason he did not. The child was thrown from the machine and sustained a fatal head injury. The coroner cleared the crew of any blame and passed a verdict of accidental death.

Cadbury Brothers Ltd decided to replace their Merryweather steamer during 1920 and purchased a brand new FE1 registered NP782 from Leyland and Company in 1921 and stationed it at their Blackpole site in Worcester. The building exists to this day and is now used by Cryo-Service Ltd. If you look at the factory you will see blue circles on the roof of the building. These are hose reels attached to high-pressure mains and were intended to fight incendiary fires on the roof of the premises. The main reason that Cadbury had such state-of-the-art machines and internal fire protection was a closely guarded secret at the time, but during both world wars the factory was used for the production of munitions for the war effort. The factories and works throughout Worcestershire have provided an important supply of additional appliances and manpower which has bolstered the local

The men of the Cadbury Works Fire Brigade at Blackpole, Worcester with the new Leyland FE1 pump, NP782 which replaced the Merryweather steamer. Clive Haynes collection

authority brigades and, as in the Norwich Union and Cadbury cases, often outshone the local brigade.

In 1921 the watch committee were again calling for the Worcester City Police Fire Brigade to replace the antiquated equipment that they had in use. The steamer, which had been proposed in 1893 and costed at £720, seems never to have arrived and it is presumed that the manual fire engine was still in use. It would take a massive blaze on 22 February 1924 at Needham and Company in Lowesmoor Wharf to provide the catalyst to buy a motor tender. The Chief Constable reported that the brigade had been called at 4.34 p.m. and responded with the horsed tender. The building in Westbury Street was found to be well alight but the brigade set to work with four lines attacking the east side of the building. The Norwich Union engine arrived shortly after and set to attacking the building from the opposite west side. The Poor Law Institution Brigade based at Tallow Hill also attended and got one hose to work. Cadbury were contacted and the new Leyland was dispatched and they soon had two lines attacking the fire. By 7.30 p.m. the fire was under control but the reputation of the Police Brigade had been severely damaged, and the building had been damaged to the tune of £8,000. It was one fire too many for the Chief Constable.

It also showed how lucky places like Stourbridge were in finding charismatic leaders like Captain Turney, who took an idea and shaped it into a reality nearly forty years earlier.

The Halesowen Volunteer Fire Brigade took delivery of a Dennis N Series pump AB9139 to replace the steamer in 1921. Les Sherlock from Bridgnorth related a very amusing story about the machine told to him by his father Fred Sherlock who

The men of Halesowen Fire Brigade outside the Cornbow Fire Station with the new Dennis pump, c.1923. Halesowen Fire Brigade

is in the picture third from the left. He was a fireman/driver who joined the brigade in 1920 and would go on to serve until 1946:

When the machine was first delivered the men from Dennis Brothers drove it around the town showing it off to the local dignitaries and the public of Halesowen. The crew sat on the running boards and the Captain of the brigade sat in the Officer's seat. When the Dennis people left for Guildford the crew were left with a shiny, impressive fire engine but, oh dear, nobody had bothered to try to drive it. The Captain told Fred that he had watched the men driving and thought he knew how to do it, so he told Fred to arrive bright and early the following morning, which was a Sunday, and they would work out how to drive it. It may sound silly but you must remember these were the early days of motorisation and they had been used to horses and steamers.

Fred and the Captain duly arrived and Fred climbed up and got the thing started. But in the jerking and kangarooing out of the station the Captain could not gain access to the vehicle and Fred couldn't stop it so they parted company. Fred decided to take it for a run and get used to it. He got really confident and put her through her paces. Eventually he decided to return to base but in those days the roads were narrow and, you guessed it, he got stuck. He persuaded a friendly farmer to give him a hand (but not before sharing in his hearty breakfast) to extract the vehicle and return to base. But luck was not on his side because soon the engine started coughing and spluttering and then died on him. Undaunted, Fred decided to walk the five miles to the Cornbow and hitch the team of fire horses and, with the assistance of a fire colleague, tow the engine back. The problem was the townspeople were now up and they witnessed the sad return of the broken down

A fine body of men outside the Mitton Street Station with the Merryweather steamer. Tom Walker

Dennis. The Captain commented: 'Hope we don't have a fire now because the horses are too damned tired after lugging that thing around!'

Though most of the new orders being placed were for motor turbines, Stourport-on-Severn UDC decided to buck the trend in 1921 and order a Merryweather Greenwich Gem steamer for the sum of £335. This machine was pulled by four horses from a local stable and was quartered originally at the Rickyard and then at the Mitton Street Station. This station provided the home for the brigade for over half a century. If you are driving through Stourport you can still see the original station shown in the picture but it now has a bricked up wall. Several nearby parishes had been approached to contribute to the costs of the steamer but Martley RDC declined to join the scheme and would not receive cover.

The Kidderminster carpet companies decided in 1923 to purchase a fire appliance for the borough that best fit their needs for up-to-date protection. NP3332, a Dennis N Series chassis, was chosen and an order was placed. The price paid was £1,560, which was a large amount of money for the period but the Dennis was now a well-proven firefighting chassis.

One of its first major fires was the massive outbreak at the Broome Mill Carpet Factory, New Road, Kidderminster on 8 December 1927. The fire, which broke out at 5.30 p.m., was still burning the following day, only being brought under control during the afternoon and 250 people lost their jobs as a consequence of the blaze. Assistance was sought from the many works brigades in the town including Jellymans (engine preserved at Bromsgrove Fire Station), Stour Vale Mills and Watson and Naylor. The fire, the biggest in forty years, caused £100,000 of damage.

The Dennis N in its pre-delivery shot at Guilford, c.1924. Transbus Dennis International Ltd

The Fire King at the Norwich Union office in Angel Place, Worcester was showing the signs of nineteen years' use during 1924 and a suitable frontline replacement was sought. Worcester had been pleased with the Fire King and sought the company's advice as to a replacement. They were advised that a good quality second-hand appliance had recently come into their possession. The 'Chemical Appliance' built in 1911 had given sterling service to the residents of the Borough of Bromley in Kent but by early 1924 was due for replacement. The quieter backwaters of Worcester would be an ideal place for the machine to retire to.

Merryweather and Sons, who had been producing manual and steam pumps for the best part of a century, also produced excellent early motorised appliances. The early Merryweather Hatfield turbine pumps were very durable and had quickly built a considerable share of the early market. The Hatfield pump delivered 300 gallons per minute while throwing a 1-inch jet to a height of 150ft. The motor built on an Aster chassis was a four-cylinder petrol engine giving a maximum speed of 30mph via three forward gears and one reverse.

In 1924 the watch committee in Worcester decided on the purchase of a 350Gpm motor tender for the Worcester City Police Fire Brigade. Records and minutes show the chassis to have been a Morris Commercial F Type but no registration number has been found. Records also show that a Bedford tender was also purchased to carry ancillary equipment. These machines were both parked in the police yard at Copenhagen Street.

Many of the smaller towns were now able to spend larger amounts of money on their own fire protection, including Evesham Borough who purchased NP4411 for their Vine Street station in 1924 to replace the old steamer.

The newly delivered Borough of Evesham Dennis N Series pump. Transbus Dennis International Ltd

During 1925 the Malvern Brigade had a review and the manual at the Wells Station was found to be obsolete. An Austin tender was purchased in 1928 and supplemented the Dennis at the main station. The Malvern Brigade could stand comparison with any brigade of its size. Malvern Museum

During 1926 the charismatic Captain Sayce of the Norwich Union Fire Brigade died and was replaced by his son A.B. Sayce. His reign would be as short as his father's had been long, as a number of issues concerning the way firefighting was carried out in Worcester were addressed. The Norwich Union Fire Brigade was disbanded in March 1929 with the Merryweather Hatfield pump LC6696 being presented to Droitwich Council. On 13 April 1929 the Merryweather Fire King FK201 was made a gift by Captain Sayce and it replaced the earlier manual pump *Niagara,* thus continuing the association of the Norwich Union in Upton-upon-Severn. This brought to an end the involvement of the Norwich Union Insurance Fire Brigade in Worcester and also nationally, as they were the last insurance brigade providing full-time cover.

A major outbreak occurred on 24 December 1925 at Hagley Hall, the residence of the Lord Lieutenant of Worcestershire, Viscount Cobham. Hagley Hall was a beautiful period house surrounded by sprawling gardens and at the time would have been considered one of the best-protected houses against fire, so what went wrong?

The weather at the time (snow and ice) had the country in an iron grip that transpired to make the hydrants and piped water freeze. The roof spaces had massive water tanks fitted but the fire was directly under one and ruptured it, causing water to pour everywhere, hampering movement but not being in sufficient quantity to quell the flames. Outside, the pools which were at the lower reaches of the park

Newly delivered to the Bromsgrove UDC in 1928 was this Leyland FE2 pump registered UY3478. This appliance replaced an earlier stop-gap FE1. As can be seen, the brigade base also housed an ambulance and an Austin car for towing the trailer pump. Also of note is the change of helmet from brass to leather. Bromsgrove Fire Station

were connected by channels to a pit near the house but the sluices which kept the water back were operated by stopcocks and due to deep drifted snow the cocks for opening them were invisible and took some locating. By the time the brigades arrived, large parts of the building were already doomed but the Stourbridge, Dudley, Kidderminster, Brierley Hill and Halesowen Brigades' suction hoses were set into water sources and at its height eleven jets were fighting the fire. As a result of excellent containment and salvage many of the priceless treasures were saved. Captain Walker assumed overall command of the incident but was injured when a floor partially collapsed. Captain Charlton of the Brierley Hill Brigade assumed command and it was he who would finally release the crews at approximately 3.30 p.m.on Christmas Day.

The appliances used at the fire were the most modern motor turbines available at the time. Brierley Hill Volunteers were using E7101, a Leyland FEI–Braidwood; Dudley Police Fire Brigade were using FD1709, also a Leyland FEI–Braidwood; the Borough of Kidderminster was using a Dennis N–Braidwood pump NP3332; the Borough of Halesowen a Dennis N–Braidwood pump AB9139; and the Stourbridge Volunteers were over the moon with their 700Gpm machine which they worked out had pumped continuously for twenty-four hours.

The Stourbridge Volunteers were starting to outgrow the old station and plans were passed for the construction of a new station opposite the existing one in Smithfield. The official opening of the new station, on 22 April 1926, was conducted by the Marquis of Cambridge in the presence of several notable dignitaries. Chief Fire Officers from Dudley, Worcester, West Bromwich, Halesowen, Cape Hill, Coventry, Birmingham and Kidderminster were also invited to a tour of the appliances and the new station's facilities.

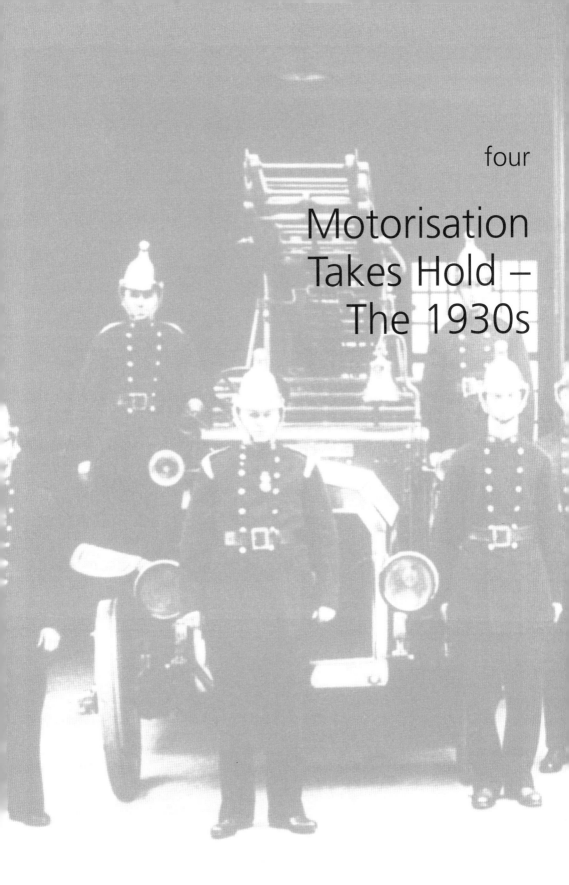

four

Motorisation
Takes Hold –
The 1930s

Some of the more enterprising machines of the times were the conversions of large cars or commercial vehicles to rudimentary fire appliances. Droitwich Spa and Pershore were two such Brigades which operated converted vehicles, in their cases a Buick Six and Wolseley Siddeley. The Buick Six was a large car of the period with a powerful six-cylinder engine capable of carrying six people and towing a trailer pump.

Not much is known about where the Buick came from or who donated it other than that it towed a 'Drysdale' trailer pump and was modified by John Morris and Company to have Braidwood bodywork fitted to the rear. The Chief Fire Officer of Droitwich at this time was well-known local businessman Joe Hunt who ran Hunts Garages in Hanbury Road on the site of the old Texaco garage.

While the large professional brigades frowned upon this 'cheap jack' type of appliance, it had much merit for the district it served. The extensive rural areas surrounding the town were entirely devoid of a piped water supply and reliance had to be placed on open water supplies for firefighting. The trailer pump (rated at 240Gpm) had the distinct advantage that it could be manhandled over the most difficult terrain to a water source to which access for a self-propelled pumping appliance was otherwise denied. The old Merryweather Hatfield it replaced was sold out of service. The Buick Six provided cover for the period up to the Second World War when the town would be provided with a Bedford Towing Vehicle. Records for the National Fire Service period in Droitwich show that a number of vehicles served in the town in a towing capacity especially during the busy Blitz period, including a Rolls Royce.

The Wolseley Siddeley motor tender of the Evesham and Pershore Rural Districts Joint Fire Brigade was based at Pershore and was donated by a Mr George Swift of Cropthorne, near Evesham. It was immediately sent to John Morris and Company in Salford for attachment of a Braidwood body. Originally purchased in 1921, it was used as a private car for twelve years before starting its second life as a fire engine in 1933. When it returned it had a Bailey wooden ladder put onto the ladder supports but due to the car having spoked wheels they found the weight of the ladder was causing the wheels to lose shape, so the top section of the ladder was removed. The appliance, like Droitwich's, towed a trailer pump, this time a Gwynne 'Invincible'. The old steamer, which had given sterling service for over a quarter of a century, was sold out of service to a scrap merchant for £10 and languished in his yard for a few years before eventually being cut up. The Wolseley was replaced in 1938 by a Morris Commercial pump.

CFO Joe Hunt and the men of the Droitwich Borough and Rural District Council Fire Brigade with their Buick Six Motor Tender, c.1930. Of special interest is the folded 'jumping sheet' on the top of the Morris Ajax ladder and the turncock standing by the trailer pump. J.O. Brettell collection

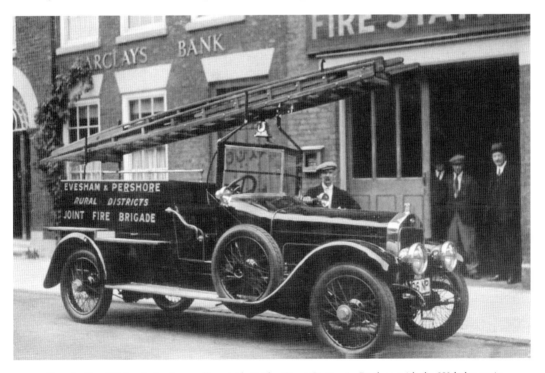

Captain Ben Hitchcock stands proudly outside Bridge Street Station in Pershore with the Wolseley on its delivery back from John Morris & Co, c.1933. E.T. Price collection

In 1929 Dennis Brothers delivered a G Series pump to the Redditch UDC. The appliance, registered UY6975, was stationed at the old station in Park Road. It was fitted with a four-cylinder petrol engine. The pump was rated at 250Gpm. This machine served right through to the fledgling Worcester City and County Fire Brigade. Transbus Dennis International Ltd

In 1928 Blockley RDC decided to replace their ageing manual pump, which had ably served the village since 1865. A fire in the village in 1926 had shown up some shortfalls in the machine, and fire is no friend to progress. The council decided to purchase a more up-to-date appliance and put out to tender. The successful bidder was Morris Commercial Cars Ltd of Birmingham who provided a popular F Series model UY4032, which was delivered on 8 September 1928. It provided much-improved pumping capacity and performance but would be lost to the county in 1931 when Blockley became part of the North Cotswolds Fire Brigade in Gloucestershire due to boundary changes.

On 8 June 1929 a fire occurred at Minchins Shop in Upton Snodsbury. The shopkeeper first phoned the Worcester then Evesham and finally Pershore Brigades but they all declined to respond as Upton Snodsbury had made no provision for fire cover. The local parishioners had to resort to the old method of throwing water onto it from a nearby well!

On 18 September 1930 a major fire occurred at the premises of T.A. Brazier Ltd on Worcester Road, Bromsgrove. Chief Officer Whyte of the Bromsgrove Fire Brigade attended and had to call on the assistance of the Kidderminster, Redditch and Droitwich Brigades for additional pumps. The fire caused £22,000 of damage and caused the closure of the factory and the laying off of the workforce.

1931 saw the Upton-upon-Severn RDC buy the six-wheeled Morris Commercial FD series machine WP689 that came complete with tank-style tracks and a Gwynne two-stage turbine pump. This machine was a monster for the time and could quite easily carry a crew of ten. It struggled to fit in the old station in New Street. The Merryweather Fire King, FK201, was sold out of service and unfortunately nothing is known of its whereabouts. The life of the Morris was somewhat short due most probably to the twin axle. Also at the end of the war

The crew under the command of Chief Officer F.J Thould sit proudly on the Morris Commercial of the Upton-upon-Severn UDC, c.1934. Note the headdress of non-peaked caps on the firemen. Upton-upon-Severn Museum

there would be a surplus of ATV type appliances. These would be able to tow the 500Gpm Coventry Climax and Dennis trailer pumps which were larger capacity and also more efficient. The second reason was most probably Health and Safety in its rudimentary form. The ATV offered a modicum of comfort and safety that the Braidwood machines lacked. 1931 also saw Droitwich Council selling off their ageing steamer to the Alcester Fire Brigade in neighbouring Warwickshire.

Another Morris Commercial was delivered in 1932, and this time the smaller F Type chassis was utilised with Braidwood-style bodywork. The Lye and Wollescote Brigade in Stourbridge decided to replace their Panhard tender, which was purchased in 1919. The appliance, registered WP1293, arrived in January and was kitted out with a 35ft Bailey ladder and other equipment. This appliance served all through the war years and was eventually withdrawn when the station was closed on the formation of the Worcester City and County Fire Brigade in 1948.

Before the war Malvern Town Brigade was under the command of George Sanders. Captain Thorpe and his Lieutenant F.C. Hemming had both retired. The 1930s heralded the arrival of a real thoroughbred fire engine: the Leyland FK1 was the premier machine of its era and Worcestershire purchased a variety of models. The first major shout that the Leyland attended was a massive fire at the laundry in Yates Hay Road in 1935.

I was contacted by 78-year-old Phyllis Hunt (*née* Hill) who was married to George Hill who was a firemen in the pre-war Malvern Brigade. She told me that 'the married men and senior officers lived in Hughendon flats in Victoria Road and they used to be alerted for calls by a bell in the flats at night or a siren mounted on the top of the nearby police station during the day'. During the war this siren would be the main air-raid warning siren for Malvern. She went on to explain 'the men used to drill on Monday nights and regularly used to drill at Hastings pool in Barnards Green'.

The main station ran WP2649, a Leyland FK1 Cub pump bought in 1932, and this machine is still in existence and currently being restored back to pristine condition by Colin Mouser in Bishops Stortford, Hertfordshire. They also ran the Dennis N as the life-saving machine with the escape ladder, which was kept alongside the pump. Chris Jackson

Above right: The second station at Grundys Lane council yard in Malvern Wells was under the command of Jim Hill. They ran the Austin Tender towing a trailer pump. This machine, like many others, would end up being used extensively in the coming Blitz of the Second World War. Clive S. Shearman collection

The newly delivered Dennis G Series pump with Captain W. Simmons and crew outside Red Lion Street, Redditch in 1933. The pump escape on the left is an earlier Dennis N Series. 'Mac' Eaton collection

During the war the Leyland and crew would regularly attend Birmingham, Coventry and London for relief calls where she said they witnessed the full horrors of the Blitz.

The new Red Lion Street Station in Redditch was erected in 1933 and replaced the cramped quarters in Alcester Street/Park Road which had served the brigade for over half a century. The new station had accommodation for six vehicles, hose drying facilities, store rooms, a recreation room and mess facilities. On the first floor the Chief Officer, Captain W Simmons, had his office. The strength of the brigade then was Captain, Second Officer (who was full-time), two firemen mechanics and eighteen retained firemen.

In the same year the Broadway, Evesham and Pershore Brigades amalgamated to form the Evesham and Pershore RDC Joint Fire Brigade. Their headquarters were at the Vine Street base in Evesham and this arrangement continued until the National Fire Service took over in 1941. Elements of the Joint Brigade attended a train crash at Ashton under Hill near Evesham on 26 February 1935. A goods train derailed on a bend and in the resultant crash the driver was killed and the locomotive fireman was seriously injured.

In 1934, under the command of Chief Constable E.W. Tinkler, policemen staffed the Worcester City Police Fire Brigade, with the only full-time fireman being Edgar 'Skipper' Pullen, who was termed a driver/policeman. He was highly qualified for the time, being a Member of the Institution of Fire Engineers (MIFE). He was in sole charge of the appliance, a Morris Commercial C Type registered FK6363, which towed a Drysdale 240Gpm trailer pump. The 35ft ladder was carried on mountings along the driver's side of the vehicle, with entry only accessible from the OIC's side.

In the early days of the Worcester City and County Fire Brigade, FK6363 was modified and converted to a self-propelled pumping appliance. A Dennis 500Gpm

Inspector Edgar 'Skipper' Pullen sits in the Officer's seat of Morris Commercial FK6363 pump of the City of Worcester Police Fire Brigade, c.1938. Ron Henderson collection

pump unit was removed from a wartime issue trailer pump and fitted to the chassis of the Morris Commercial, the pump being energised from the road engine. The ladder gantries were removed from the offside of the appliance and replaced by new overhead gantries in order to carry the ladder in a more conventional position.

In the City of Worcester numerous hydrants were installed, spaced approximately 250 feet apart. Where no immediate building or structure was available to fix a hydrant indicator plate, the Corporation provided a unique marker post, manufactured from cast iron. A small number are still in existence to this day. They comprise a spiral post approximately 5ft tall, set in the roadside verge. There are examples on the Droitwich Road, near Perdiswell Park and the Bransford Road, near Kay and Company. In 1938 the Worcester City Police Fire Brigade answered about forty calls a year at a cost of £1,300.

By the mid-1930s the last manuals and steamers were disappearing from service. Bewdley Borough Council decided in 1935 that a replacement was necessary and a Bedford WLG-chassied pump which had been used as a demonstrator by the company was purchased. This appliance, registered AMY433, towed a trailer pump.

Tenbury Wells was one of the last brigades in the region to see its steamer disappear. But what arrived to replace it, a Leyland FK6 Cub, CAB650, was the Rolls Royce of fire appliances. The Leyland FK6 was a six-cylinder, petrol-engined machine with Tenbury Wells' example having the safer 'New World'-styled body. A Tenbury Wells fireman had been killed in a freak accident after being thrown off the steamer while on the way to a fire and this may have had a bearing on the decision.

One of the major fires of the period was at Witley Court, the residence of Sir Herbert Smith who was one of the rich carpet manufacturers of the time. The fire occurred on the evening of 7 September 1937 and the first calls were received at approximately 8 p.m., with the first appliances arriving about twenty minutes later. Appliances attended from the Stourport-on-Severn, Stourbridge, Kidderminster, Bromsgrove, Malvern and Worcester City Police Fire Brigades. They immediately set their suction hoses into the vast lake and continued to pump for many hours. The fire had by this time been lost and the crews set about containment and salvage. It resulted in large parts of the stately home being destroyed and priceless treasures being lost for ever. Witley Court was renowned for its beautiful fountains, which required an enormous amount of pressure to operate and a hydrant system had been installed but unfortunately these had been allowed to fall into disrepair. Also there were stories of engines becoming bogged down near the pool while pumping and having to be removed by tractor. The following morning dawned to show a scene of total devastation with Witley Court shrouded in smoke and ninety per cent of the building totally destroyed. September 1937 turned into a bad month for fire loss in the United Kingdom. The total loss was put at £1.6 million, with the fire at Witley Court contributing £500,000.

Dennis Brothers of Guilford were still producing premier fire appliances and provided the popular 'Ace' model to Bromsgrove in 1935 and Stourport-on-Severn in 1937. These models came with the 'New World'-styled body providing better crew protection inside the machine than the earlier Braidwood style, which had the crew facing outwards with the emphasis on holding on tight. Fatalities were common with firemen falling off while getting dressed, being knocked off or with the appliance crashing on the way to jobs. The Dennis Ace, delivered to Stourport-on-Severn in 1937, had a four-cylinder petrol-driven engine powering a Dennis

Dennis Brothers also produced this New World-bodied Ace for Stourport-on-Severn UDC. Transbus Dennis International Ltd

The Dennis Ace pump BUY353 outside the Mitton Street Station in Stourport. Yvonne Smith collection

350Gpm pump. This machine would serve well into the 1950s at the Mitton Street Station, eventually being sold out of service in 1959.

The Stourbridge Fire Brigade was involved in two contrasting occasions during the mid-1930s. A very happy event took place on Saturday 15 June 1935 with the marriage of Mr Anthony Bickerton Brown, a member of the brigade, to Miss Dorothy Merrick Blagbrough at St Thomas's Church, Stourbridge. This was a full ceremonial wedding with everybody in full uniform under the command of Captain T.L. Walker and Deputy W.H. Meredith who headed a group of firemen forming an arch of axes. The bride was then driven to the reception on the ribbon-bedecked Dennis with the appliance, a Morris Commercial from Lye and Wollescote, providing musical accompaniment in the form of the bell being rung vigorously.

The second occasion was the sad death of Captain Hughes of the Kidderminster Brigade in May 1937. Captain Hughes had been an inspirational leader for thirty-two years and had shaped the brigade into a respected force. Mourners from all over the country attended and he had a full ceremonial funeral. His helmet and axe were placed on his coffin, which was draped with a Union Jack and then taken on Kidderminster Borough's Dennis to the church. Many brigades followed the funeral cortège, slowly marching behind their station's appliance. It made for a very impressive but solemn sight, and also demonstrated how close the fire service family was in Worcestershire.

Above and right: *The maids of honour are brought to the ceremony on the Lye appliance Morris Commercial F Type WP1293 and the arch of honour at church for Anthony Bickerton Brown and Miss Dorothy Merrick Blagborough's wedding in 1935.* Yvonne Smith collection

Right and below: *The funeral of the respected Captain Hughes of the Kidderminster Fire Brigade in 1937. The Stourbridge Brigade march to the church and the coffin is carried by the crew of the Kidderminster Brigade.* Yvonne Smith collection

five

Dangerous Times Ahead

Injury and death are the constant companions of firefighters as the Stourbridge Volunteers found out when they were called to a fire at United Supper Services in Stourbridge on 13 February 1937. The fire involved a number of fryers and a cooker. The fryers had spilled their contents over some gas couplings which had melted and produced a jet of flaming gas like a flame-thrower across the kitchen. Captain Walker assumed command of the incident and sent a crew to find the stopcock for the gas supply and directed other crews to fight the fire. As the crew was leaving the rear of the premises to find the stopcock there was an enormous explosion, which blew out the back and front of the premises. There must have been a build up of the gas which had just required a spark to ignite it. Nine members of the crew were injured with three receiving injuries requiring attendance overnight in the Corbett Hospital in Stourbridge. An interesting entry in *The Fireman* magazine of 1939 notes that Captain Walker had just completed sixty years in the brigade, joining in 1879 when he was twenty years old.

The next Leyland, purchased in 1936, went to Oldbury Metropolitan Borough to replace the FE1 purchased in 1920. The Leyland FK6, AWP486, was a six-cylinder variant fitted with a 500Gpm pump and served at the Tower and Perrott Street Stations.

The largest fire to occur on Oldbury's patch during the 1930s happened on 22 August 1932 when the brigade were summoned to a fire at Lench Ltd of Blackheath. There were reports that two oil tanks containing 3,000 gallons of crude oil were on fire and there were fears of an imminent explosion. The brigade, under Superintendant Challinor, responded and were quickly on scene. The fire proved difficult to contain and assistance was requested with the Rowley Regis, West Bromwich, Dudley Police FB, Tipton, Halesowen, Tividale and Cape Hill Brewery Brigades responding. After six exhausting hours the fire was brought under control. The total bill for the fire damage was estimated as being in excess of £30,000.

The Kidderminster Fire Brigade was called to another major fire at the Brintons Wool and Spinning Mill on 24 February 1937. Assistance was sought from the Stourport-on-Severn, Stourbridge, Bromsgrove and Worcester City Police FB. The damage from the fire was put in the region of £5,000.

Stourbridge Borough had operated the Dennis N Series as its primary life-saving appliance since 1916 and by the late 1930s it was starting to show its age. Tenders were put out, with Leyland being the successful bidder. A Leyland FKT9 Tiger was delivered to the brigade in 1940 and very quickly earned its spurs. As with the other local brigades, appliances that would have been sold out of service or even scrapped were retained as the situation in Europe spiralled out of control.

The Leyland FT9 which was delivered to Stourbridge Borough in 1940 is shown shortly after the war following the birth of the Worcester City and County Brigade. Stourbridge Library

The proud men of Oldbury Metropolitan Borough with their Leyland FK6 on its delivery in 1936. Dr Terry Daniels

Captain Ben Hitchcock and his men with the newly delivered Morris Commercial pump in 1938.
George Hitchcock collection

1938 saw Captain Ben Hitchcock receive a Morris Commercial, CAB992, which was delivered to the Evesham and Pershore Joint RDC for use at the Bridge Street Station. The pump was delivered with the old fashioned Braidwood seating arrangement. The Wolseley was disposed of and the trailer pump passed to the Broadway Fire Brigade.

Captain Hitchcock had been a stickler for the brigade always looking smart. This was the mark of the man and his men were respected around the town for their professional approach. But his adherence to this policy would backfire dramatically during the coming Blitz that heralded the start of the Second World War. On several trips to Birmingham, Coventry and Plymouth the brigade were mobilised to fight the conflagrations and the townsfolk would see the gleaming Morris leave the station with the neatly attired firemen and wave them off. Days later they would see the same clean vehicle arrive back. The returning firemen would gather in the local pubs and recount their tales of fires out of control and the ever-present threat of death and destruction. The townsfolk could not believe how clean the men were on their return, but unbeknown to them, Captain Hitchcock was stopping on the return journey so that the crew could clean the machine and themselves before re-entering Pershore. The crew decided to remedy the situation and after a heavy raid in Swansea they returned without stopping to clean themselves up. They looked like a group of black and white minstrels on the fire engine that looked like a coal truck but oh, did they get a reception! They were treated like returning heroes and were again the toast of the town.

Captain Hitchcock served right through the war years and guided his brigade into the Worcester City and County Fire Brigade. He finally retired during the 1950s. Unfortunately, some influential former Captains and Chief Officers would pass away during the National Fire Service period, among them A.B. Sayce (Norwich Union), F.J. Thould (Upton-upon-Severn) and Thomas Walker (Stourbridge).

Halesowen Borough purchased a Leyland FK8 model DAB407 in 1939 as a replacement for the earlier Dennis but with the war looming they decided to run the two at the Great Cornbow.

Les Sherlock's sister, who used to go to the station with her father, has fond memories of the arrival of the Leyland. 'I remember cleaning the brasswork on *Tilly*, the older Dennis, but the newer Leyland had only chrome fittings and I didn't think it was as fine'. But as a fire engine it was a major step up, possessing a 500Gpm pump compared to the 350Gpm pump on the earlier machine.

Like all firemen of this period, Fred Sherlock and the men of the Halesowen Brigade would face the full horror of war close up, fighting the Blitz fires. Les Sherlock's sister remembers 'scraping burned flesh off his fire tunic with a knife' and also finding out only on the following morning that, on a couple of occasions, he had been hospitalised as a result of injuries sustained while firefighting. 'That was the worrying time when they would go off to fires and you would hear a crew had been killed and in all the confusion nobody would know who it was until they had returned home the next morning.'

But not all the stories are bad! 'They came back from one fire in Birmingham with an extra crew member, Blitz the wirehaired terrier. He was found wandering the streets and came back with the crew and from that day on would attend every shout, sitting himself next to the OIC. At the end of hostilities the crew were

This premier firefighting machine was a Leyland FK8, delivered from Leyland Motors to fight fires in Halesowen, Worcestershire during 1939. John C. Thompson collection

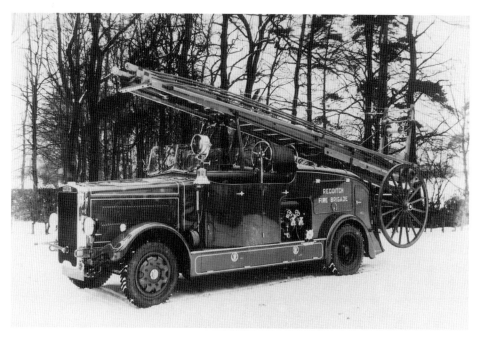

This Leyland FKT2 differed from the Halesowen FK8 in that it had the safer transverse seating accommodation. This machine was delivered to the Redditch Fire Brigade to replace the earlier Dennis N Series pump escape. John C. Thompson collection

This Leyland FKT2 had the safer transverse seating accommodation. This view also shows the 50ft wheeled escape. This was the fire service's main piece of life saving equipment. The shot shows it after it had transferred to Worcester City and County Fire Brigade. 'Mac' Eaton collection

presented to HRH Prince of Wales, who gave them all medals and, you've guessed it, Blitz also got one!'

At the end of the Blitz the old Dennis, AB9139, was finally stood down and sold out of service.

In 1940 Redditch Fire Brigade needed a replacement for the Dennis N pump escape and after a number of tenders ordered a Leyland FKT2 model with the transverse seating arrangement. The machine was delivered to Red Lion Street on 20 January 1940. The chief officer at the time, L.O. Wilkes, gave the machine a test drive and must have been impressed by it. The pump escape was the main rescue appliance at fires and with a new 50ft 'Ajax' escape ladder, was the high-rise appliance in the town. The Dennis, which had served the town since 1910, was retained like so many other machines of its vintage due to the war. That these machines were still serving brigades up and down the country thirty years after attending their first shout also served as testimony to the original build quality of Dennis Brothers!

In January 1941 call bells were introduced into the Redditch firemen's houses and this gave the chief the ability to reduce the amount of time crews had to spend on standby. The crews were divided into two watches, each taking a daily and a nightly turn at reporting for duty. In 1941 there were eight full-time firemen and thirteen retained men.

The Fire Brigade Bill – 1938

During 1938 a Bill was introduced into Parliament to make further provision for fire services in Great Britain. Previously the responsibility for organising brigades had been vested in Borough, Urban and Parish Councils. Borough and Urban Councils were to remain as Fire Authorities but the responsibility of Parish Councils was to be repealed and transferred to District Councils.

All Fire Authorities were to be placed under a statutory obligation to make provision for the organisation of the protection of life and property in case of fire,

Typical of the type of AFS towing vehicles around was this little Ford Model T. The trailer pump is a 350Gpm Coventry Climax. The conversion work was carried out by Kidderminster firemen, c.1939. C. Wooldridge collection

by securing efficient fire services for their districts, either by maintaining a fire brigade themselves or by entering into arrangements with another fire authority to maintain cover. All fire authorities were empowered to enter into arrangements with water undertakers for securing an adequate supply of water in case of fire.

Many other important changes and duties were to be imposed, including one very positive and outstanding directive, the removal of the imposition of charges by Fire Authorities on occupiers of property for the attendance of the brigade to extinguish any outbreak of fire. Generally, the provisions of the Bill were far reaching and indicated a forward-thinking and progressive attitude. A Fire Service Commission was also to be established to review the new authorities, with the power to punish the defaulters by removing their control and empowering an emergency Fire Board to run the authority.

The outline of the Bill was welcomed by both houses and, with minor amendments, quickly passed though the varied Parliamentary and Committee stages. It received Royal Assent on 27 August 1938 and became the Fire Brigades Act 1938.

The Auxillary Fire Service (AFS) – 1938

The growing tensions and increasing hostility in central Europe had persuaded the government to prepare for imminent war. Under the provisions of the Air Raid Precautions Act, the government had decided to place large orders with pump manufacturers for the supply of trailer pumps. These, together with hose and associated equipment, were to be issued free of charge to Local Authorities. In addition, large numbers of civilians were to be recruited into the Auxillary Fire Service and given sixty hours' basic training. The responsibility for the provision of towing vehicles for the pumps was left to individual authorities in the first instance, with the proviso that should the need arise large cars and small goods vehicles would be commandeered from the general public, and adapted for the purpose of towing vehicles.

Little fire sub-stations were set up at a variety of locations; within Worcester City there were sub-stations in London Road, Sebright Drive, Chapel Walk, Bull Entry and Pitmaston Road, St Johns. (For more information please refer to list in the Appendix). While work had been started on the construction of the large fire station in Copenhagen Street, which was originally designed to provide residential accommodation for the police on the upper floors above the garaging for the fire appliances and police vehicles, this station was not ready for occupation until late in 1942.

It was estimated during January 1938 that some 20,000 pumps were available on call in the United Kingdom. By this time the AFS personnel had been issued with a cap, overalls, rubber boots and a steel helmet. They would have to wait a while longer before waterproof leggings and a fire tunic were issued. Women were recruited to drive staff cars and trained to undertake watch-room and control duties. For control and administrative purposes the country was divided into nineteen Civil Defence Regions.

The Outbreak of Hostilities – 1939

The Luftwaffe had bombed Spain to its knees and the powers that be saw the same coming for Britain. There was no co-ordinated approach to firefighting at this time – neighbouring brigades often used different sized hose couplings. The close spacing of individual hydrants in many moderately sized towns and cities provides evidence that initial firefighting relied on a line of hose and a jet from a street hydrant. This may be seen to be the case in the older parts of Worcester where early installed hydrants are spaced approximately 250ft apart. Malvern Town used a form of pillar hydrant located in the base of the street gas lamp standards.

With the declaration war with Germany all firemen and the AFS were instructed to report for duty at their respective stations. At this instant all of the fire stations became manned on a full-time basis. This threw up an immense problem of providing suitable accommodation for the personnel, as all of the stations within Worcestershire had previously operated on a part-time or volunteer basis with only basic facilities available. In the ensuing weeks prefabricated huts were hastily erected on any available land surrounding stations to provide the necessary additional accommodation. It was perhaps fortunate that apart from a few isolated incidents the expected heavy bombing raids did not occur during the first year of the 'Phoney War'. This afforded the opportunity for full-scale exercises to be carried out and some of the many shortcomings of the enlarged and disjointed fire service as a whole to be corrected.

1940

During August 1940 the first concentrated enemy air raids began, giving a foretaste of what was to follow. The Surrey Commercial Docks of East London were the initial target. Enormous areas were destroyed by fire, some fire 'zones' requiring the attendance of more than 100 pumps. The heavy raids on London continued for more than forty consecutive nights. During this period, under the reinforcement scheme, pumps from Worcestershire were dispatched to assist in the provision of fire cover for London and the crews undertaking relief duty.

By September 1940 fifty AFS personnel had been killed and 500 injured. The heavy raids then switched to Coventry and in a long, sustained attack, reduced the city to a mass of flames. Pumps from Worcestershire were dispatched to assist. Raids then rapidly switched to other major industrialised cities and ports throughout England and Wales. In a number of instances, pumps from Worcestershire were active in support, often travelling many miles. Although the towns within Worcestershire were not directly targeted in any mass air raid, stray aircraft picked opportunist targets. The Meco works in Worcester was bombed on 3 October, resulting in massive damage and the loss of seven lives. By the end of the Blitz it was estimated that nearly 800 bombs and 8,000 incendiary devices had hit the county. Locally, the small brigades who covered the busy RAF airfields at Honeybourne, Defford, Bishampton and Perdiswell regularly attended incidents involving crashed aircraft and associated loss of life.

The Coventry Blitz – 14 and 15 November 1940

Many of the local Worcestershire stations sent machines all over the South-West and Midlands to conflagrations during the Blitz period but the incident which stood out in most recollections was the Coventry Blitz.

The City of Coventry Fire Brigade began receiving warning messages at 7.05 p.m., with the final red warning of imminent attack received at 7.10 p.m. The moonlit night sky was very clear and in the first attack a large gas main was ruptured and this provided a beacon for the raiders to home in on. Fifty-six calls were recorded in the first half-hour and many of these required in excess of five pumps each. The fires were reported across six districts and pumps were mobilised and column officers were tasked with giving early reports of the size and nature of the fire and the situation as regards reinforcements.

The workhorse of the National Fire Service was the trailer pump. Various makes were available, Coventry Climax, Dennis, Beresford, Drysdale and Gwynne to mention a few. These auxiliary firemen are using Dennis pumps at the rear of Castle Road Station, Kidderminster in the 1940s. C. Wooldridge collection

At 7.59 p.m. it was realised that this raid was out of the ordinary and all the local resources were committed. By now seventy calls had been received and incendiaries, parachute mines, oil bombs and high explosive bombs were falling all across the city. To add to the difficulties, the headquarters in Hales Street received a direct hit and a fire was started in the roof, necessitating the evacuation of the control room. Extra turntable ladders were requested along with three heavy water relaying units as water supplies became exhausted. Water dams had been set up along the River Sherbourne and these proved invaluable as many pumps called to stop and replenish supplies at these and the many swimming pools and ornamental pools which had been earmarked.

At 8.47 p.m. most of the telephone lines were out of order so the messenger service came into its own. At 11.15 p.m. a request was sent for an additional forty pumps and senior officers to replace the ones killed and injured. All the incoming out-of-area crews were allocated a messenger to direct them in the unfamiliar surroundings, but many crews just came upon conflagrations and so set to work. The fires in the centre of the city eventually joined to make a massive inferno and orders were given to withdraw and surround. Unfortunately, some of the local crews were the first to be killed and injured and this very soon had a knock-on effect. Refreshment and reliefs were virtually impossible in the early hours of the attack so exhaustion was commonplace, but the spirits of the crew never wavered. The local works brigades in the city kept damage to their own factories to a minimum and they also provided invaluable assistance to the local crews.

During the raid (up to the point when the telephone lines failed) 204 fires were recorded, but the number was most probably double that. Many appliances were seriously damaged and some were destroyed. The number of firemen killed was twenty-six, with over 200 injured, thirty-four seriously. (Report by W.H. Cartwright, MIFE, Chief Officer, City of Coventry Fire Brigade.)

1941

Despite the preparation for war, there were many shortcomings and an urgent need was foreseen for vast improvement in the organisation of the Fire Service throughout the whole of the country. Standardisation in the equipping and training of personnel was considered essential. The War Cabinet agreed to the principle of a nationalised fire brigade and a Bill to form the National Fire Service was presented to Parliament and passed though all its stages, receiving Royal Assent on 22 May. Under the Fire Services (Emergency Provisions) Act 1941, powers were conferred on the Secretary of State to provide by regulation for the period of the emergency, the co-ordination and control of the Fire Services of the United Kingdom. The NFS came into being on 18 August 1941 and reorganisation began immediately. The Secretary of State gave an undertaking that the Fire Service would be returned to Local Authority control once hostilities had ceased.

six

Worcestershire at War – National Fire Service 1941-1945

Under the control of the NFS the country was divided into thirty-two Fire Force regions, twenty-six in England and Wales and six in Scotland. Each was to be under the authority of a Fire Force Commander and his assistant. The area of each Fire Force was divided into divisions, the size being related to the assessed risk and each division falling under the command of a Divisional Officer, who was responsible for 100 pumps. The division was further divided into two companies, each of fifty pumps, under the command of a Company Officer. The companies were further divided into five columns, under the command of a Column Officer, responsible for ten pumps. Each pump would have a Leading Fireman in Charge. Such organisation enabled the mass movement of pumps, with an effective supervisory officer structure.

The whole of Worcestershire, Warwickshire and Herefordshire came under the auspices of Fire Force 23 and 24 (parts later merged into 23).

South Worcestershire came under A1 Division, Herefordshire A2, Warwickshire was divided into B1 and B2 Divisions and North Worcestershire similarly divided into C1 and C2 Divisions.

The National Fire Service headquarters for Worcestershire were located at Bevere Manor, on the outskirts of Worcester. The person appointed as head of Fire Force 23 was Fire Force Commander A.J. Bridle, who was later succeeded by C.M. Kerr in September 1943.

Fire Force Area 23 included the County Borough of Worcester, the Boroughs of Bewdley, Droitwich, Evesham and Kidderminster, the Urban Districts of Malvern and Stourport-on-Severn and the Rural Districts of Droitwich, Evesham, Kidderminster, Martley, Pershore, Tenbury and Upton-upon-Severn.

Fire Force Area 24 included the Boroughs of Halesowen, Oldbury and Stourbridge, the Urban Districts of Bromsgrove and Redditch and the Rural District of Bromsgrove. These areas were later amalgamated into Fire Force Area 23.

Pebworth by this time had received a Coventry Climax trailer pump, towed by an Austin 12 car. The car was later replaced with a Ford V8 Pilot. During 1942 and the newly formed NFS, Pebworth fire station was given the identification B12(f), coming under the control of the Leamington Division. Pebworth was later supplied with an Austin K2 towing vehicle and a Dennids trailer pump. To accomodate this appliance a utility building, comprising corrugated sheet metal supported on a scaffold pole framework, was erected in Station Lane.

A wartime shot of the C2Z Ideal Garage (Hopwood) AFS sub-station crew being inspected by a dignitary. The towing vehicle was most likely a taxi. 'Mac' Eaton collection

The National Fire Service Fleet

All appliances were delivered in NFS grey paint, and all existing appliances had their red coachwork and chrome and brass fittings painted over. Headlamps were covered to protect against the blackout. The Home Office placed an order for 2,000 Austin K2 towing vehicles, to replace the worn out lorries and cars currently being used. All Home Office issue appliances, however austere, were provided with a crew cab.

Many parishes organised their own fire parties. Inkberrow operated a Coventry Climax light trailer pump towed to incidents by local man Desmond Savage. Clifton on Teme also had a Coventry Climax trailer pump, this time towed by the vicar's car. Station Officer Maund from Tenbury Wells was in overall charge. Sid Gittins, a local haulier in Wychbold, allowed one of his lorries to act as a towing vehicle for ARP duties. In Fernhill Heath near Worcester local man Bob Carr used a Singer car to tow a trailer pump. This arrangement was typical of the spirit of the time.

Under the auspices of the NFS, while there were a number of appliances and ancillary vehicles allocated to specialist duty, the principal vehicles in the fleet included:

Heavy Unit: six deliveries, output 700Gpm. This pump was a self-contained unit, mounted at the rear of a lorry chassis. Crew cab and equipment lockers.
Extra Heavy Unit: six deliveries, output 1,000Gpm. same set-up as above.
Towing Vehicle (ATV): A 2-ton box van, having steel sides and a reinforced splinter-proof roof. Crew seats were lift-up lockers. Canvas curtains covered the rear.
Light trailer pump: one delivery, output 140 – 180Gpm
Medium trailer pump: two deliveries, output 300 – 350Gpm
Large trailer pump: two deliveries, output 450 – 500Gpm

This light trailer pump was built by Coventry Climax and was towed behind Worcester's escape carrying unit Fordson 7V GLD147.
Malvern Museum

This large trailer pump was built by Coventry Climax and was towed behind Worcester's Austin ATV GLT655.
Malvern Museum

A Leyland TD7 with a Merryweather 100ft ladder GLW428 was delivered to the county and was allocated to Copenhagen Street in Worcester. This was the first aerial appliance in the county and would be followed later by a Leyland TSC Beaver, also with a Merryweather ladder, which was allocated to Kidderminster.

The incidents of the NFS period showed that mobilisation and command and control were the way forward. There were large fires at Lancaster Ltd, Worcester and Carpet Trades Ltd, Kidderminster in 1942, which would have swamped the pre-war brigades. Now the emphasis was on a more structured fire service better suited to the times. A later fire at the Deanery, Worcester in 1943 showed the advantages of having a turntable ladder to protect the city.

As time progressed there were many adaptations and improvements in appliance design. From the Home Office fleet, perhaps two types of appliance should be singled out as they pioneered the forerunners of today's modern appliance. The escape carrying unit, later to be termed a pump escape was, with its rudimentary

Leyland Beaver/Merryweather Turntable Ladder GXA63 in its NFS livery and also sporting its NFS code 23B TL1. Ron Henderson collection

23A Worcester had a new headquarters in 1942 with the opening of the Deansway Station, and this Fordson 7V escape carrying unit was delivered to serve there. Note the trailer carrying the light pump. Malvern Museum

Austin K4 Escape Carrying Unit operating out of Howsell Road, Malvern, c.1960. This machine had served at Malvern since the Second World War. It originally towed a trailer pump on a rigid bar but had now been modified to carry a Barton front mounted pump. Ian Moore collection

form of limousine bodywork, the nearest recognisable appliance to that of its pre-war counterpart. This class of appliance was the only Home Office issue that was provided with hose reel equipment. The early models also towed a large trailer pump attached to a long rigid bar in order that the towed pump would clear the large escape wheels. Problems arose with the tow bar bending out of shape. Additionally, the trailer had to be unhitched before the escape ladder could be slipped from its mountings. These problems were later overcome by installing an American 'Barton' front drive pump with an output of 350Gpm. The pump was fitted forward of the vehicle radiator and driven directly from the prime mover crankshaft, via a clutch. The modified appliance now became a self-contained unit.

Perhaps two distinctly different appliances are worthy of mention. For the first time the busy inland ports of the river Severn were supplied with fireboats, based at Stourport-on-Severn and Worcester. These units comprised a converted trawler and cruiser respectively, fitted with extra heavy pumps and a deck mounted monitor. They could both operate as an independent firefighting unit, or be used to pump water ashore via hose lines for large relaying purposes.

Previously, the repair and maintenance of pumps and vehicles had caused immense problems. The NFS opened a centralised workshop at Padmore Street, Worcester, staffed by mechanics and engineers from within the service.

Probably the most innovative and significant appliance to be developed from the Home Office stable was the water tender. This started life as a mobile dam unit, a lorry fitted with a large water tank, used to ferry water from any available source to refill emergency dams that had been erected in strategic locations.

Subsequently, by mounting a light pump behind the tank and equipping with hose and associated equipment, this appliance could operate as a self-contained unit to deal with moderately sized fires. Its usefulness in remote and rural areas became particularly significant. This rudimentary appliance, with development and many adaptions, became the basis of the modern appliance of today.

As you will see, after the end of hostilities these machines provided the backbone of the fleet which would become the fledgling Worcester City and County Fire Brigade.

Shortly after the inception of the National Fire Service the heavy air raids abated, Germany now concentrating its assault on eastern Europe although isolated raids still occurred. The Fire Service in Worcestershire was not idle – fires still broke out, some of large and serious proportions. Fires involving industrial buildings or armament production or which were directly connected with the war effort were not made public, owing to reporting restrictions. Everyday fires involving domestic property still occurred, some with tragic loss of life. Many large fires happened on farms among harvested and stored crop. During the long period of preparation for the invasion of northern France a number of crews (codename Operation Colourscheme) from Worcestershire were sent to assist in providing protection for the huge military depots and encampments which were concentrated all over southern England, prior to the launch of the Normandy Invasion.

One of the survivors of the National Fire Service period is this Austin K4-Merryweather 60ft mechanical ladder which was supplied to Kidderminster. The appliance is now preserved by Chris Tallents of Highley. Clive S. Shearman collection

Howsell Road, Malvern with the Austin PE and Austin ATV, c.1950. Worcester City and County Fire Brigade archive

Charles T. Hill, who formerly served with the National Fire Service at the Merton Road station in Malvern Link, told me that 'there was a temporary wooden four-storey drill tower built in the field next door to the Malvern Technical School near to the Victoria Road Station. This was used for escape practice and hose drying.' Charles went on to serve at Howsell Road, Malvern with the Worcester City and County Fire Brigade.

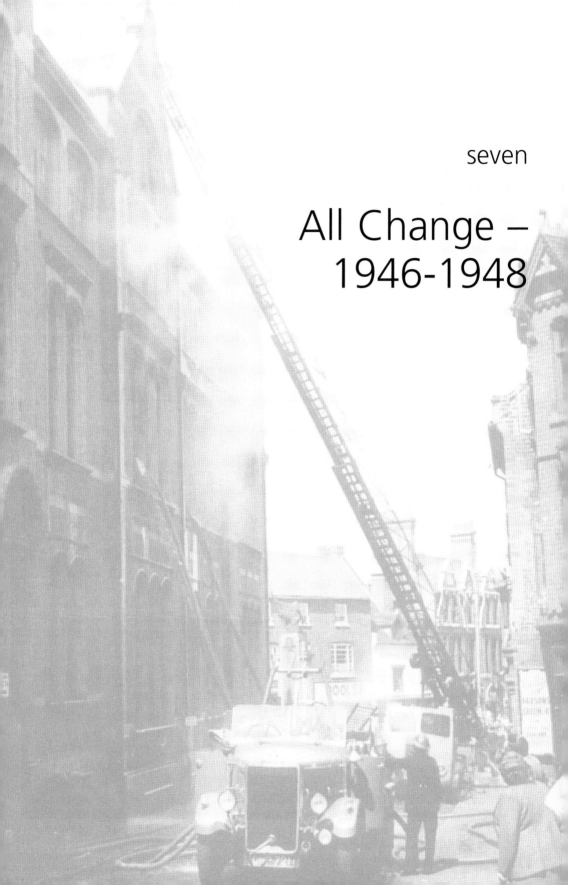

seven

All Change –
1946-1948

At the end of the hostilities the majority of the satellite fire stations were closed and many of the full-time staff returned to their former occupations. However, Worcester, Kidderminster, Stourbridge, Halesowen, Oldbury, Bromsgrove, Redditch, Evesham and Malvern would continue to remain continuously manned, also being supported as required by retained personnel. The remainder of the county stations were operated by retained staff.

The last large-scale mobilisation of NFS appliances occurred following the severe winter of 1947 when, after a sudden thaw, many parts of south-east England suffered enormous and devastating flooding. A total of 600 pumps and support appliances were sent to assist in that area from all parts of the country, including many from various parts of Worcestershire.

During 1947 the Fire Services Act was published to return the responsibility for the fire brigade to local authority control on 1 April 1948. There was, however, a sting in the tail: County Councils and County Borough Councils were to become the new authorities. The new brigades were to be reduced in number from 1,400 pre-war, to just 140. The Home Office was to have overall control relating to standards, including prescribed standards of fire cover for specific areas of risk, the number of men and appliances that would form the initial attendance to any fire and time limits for such attendances. The Act imposed many exacting requirements in respect of establishments, training, water supplies and arrangements for mutual assistance between adjoining brigades. It also forbade the formation of Police Fire Brigades or any policeman becoming a member of a fire brigade.

There were two chains of command, firstly the Fire Department at the Home Office and secondly, the Fire and Public Protection Committee of the County or County Borough Council. Under the provisions of the Fire Services Act, Worcester City and Worcestershire County Council were empowered to become Fire Authorities in their own right. Owing to the overall size of each authority, agreement was reached to form a combination scheme entitled the Worcester City and County Fire Brigade. From the city and county representatives selected to serve on the Fire Brigade Committee, Alderman Amphlett was elected as chairman and Brigadier Brittain as vice-chairman.

The first task facing the Committee was to select, from a shortlist of suitable applicants, a Chief Fire Officer. Gerald Eastham was chosen to fill the post. Prior to the war he had served as Third Officer in the Preston County Borough Brigade. He had served with the army overseas' contingent of the National Fire Service, attaining the rank of Lieutenant Colonel, and had later returned to 23 Fire Force of

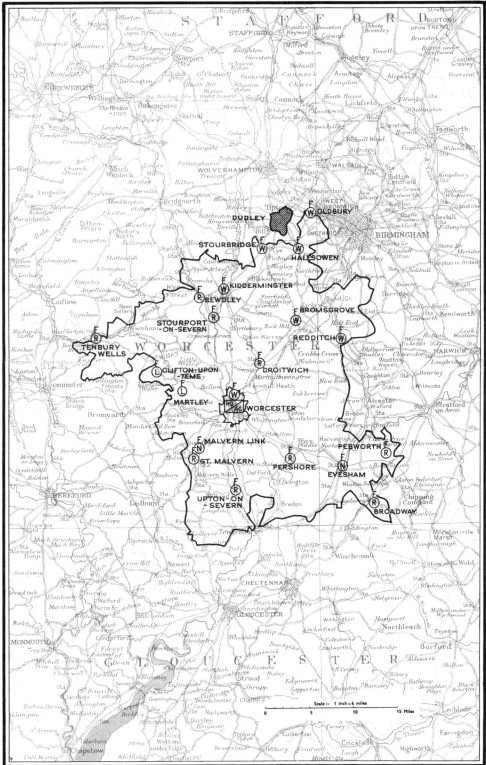

Scale :- 1 inch = 6 miles

0   5   10   15 Miles

the NFS in the rank of Column Officer. Aged thirty-six, he was the youngest Chief Officer in the country. Mr J.W. Sanders from Bristol was appointed DCFO, to be followed by Mr F. Boulter, who would later be appointed CFO (Chief Fire Officer) of Oxford in 1962.

Prior to the formation of the new Fire Authorities, the Home Office determined exacting standards relating to the number and disposition of appliances required to respond to fires in all areas of the country. Also the basic standards were set for the manufacture and type of fire appliances to be maintained, at the same time allowing scope for further improvement and development. A committee comprising representatives of the Home Office Engineering Department, the Chief Officers, the Fire Brigades Union and the Institution of Fire Engineers was established, to form the Joint Committee for Design and Development (JCDD). Exacting minimum standards were set regarding engine size, attainable speed, brake efficiency and pump capacity, in addition to many other salient features including the nature of minimum equipment to be carried.

These early specifications related to appliances comprising pumps, pump escapes, water tenders and emergency tenders. At that time it was recognised that financial restrictions and availability of new commercial chassis would pose problems for a number of years, therefore allowance was made for the upgrading of ex-NFS vehicles. A specification was established to upgrade Austin K2 towing vehicles, for the fitting of a 60-gallon water tank, a small pump driven from the gearbox power take off, and the provision of a hose reel.

In order for the water tender to be categorised as a pump, it was necessary for that class of appliance to tow a large trailer pump. This often posed a problem as many pre-war stations were not large enough to house such lengthy appliances, yet poor area water supply dictated otherwise. CFO Gerald Eastham had other ideas. He pioneered the fitting of a major pump to the chassis of an existing ex-Home Office water tender, the pump being driven from the road engine. He took the idea to the Home Office and won the day, which led to the specification of the water tender (type B) or pump water tender, as it became familiarly known. With the aid of the Brigade Workshop staff and local coachbuilder Carmichael, a number of the new specification appliances were added to the fleet.

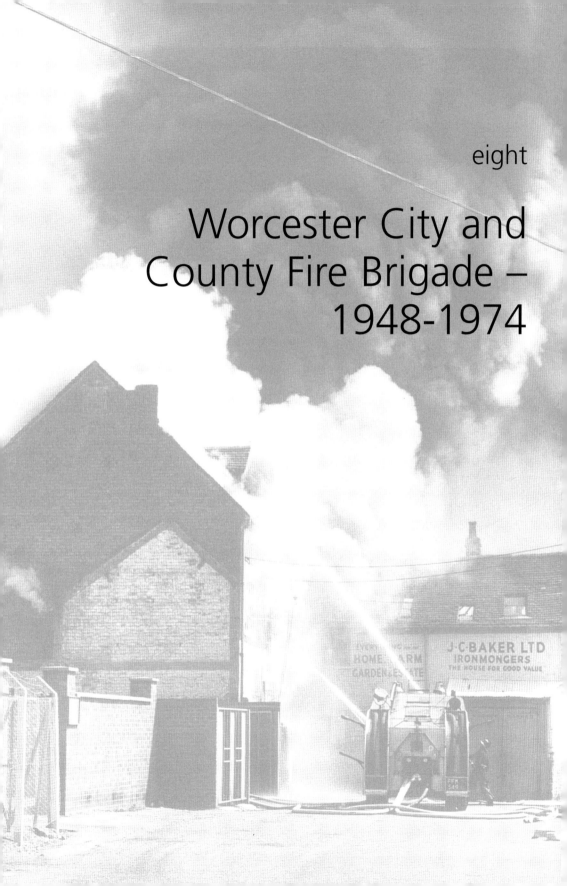

eight

Worcester City and County Fire Brigade – 1948-1974

The new authority comprised two divisions, South Division HQ and Fire Control, based at the Copenhagen Street Fire Station in Worcester, and North Division HQ and Sub Fire Control, based at the Castle Road, Kidderminster Fire Station. Full-time stations, all having a retained establishment, included Worcester, Evesham, Malvern, Kidderminster, Stourbridge, Halesowen, Oldbury, Bromsgrove and Redditch. The remainder were single-pump retained stations, with the exception of Stourport-on-Severn and Tenbury Wells, which were two-pump stations.

Lye and Malvern Wells closed almost immediately. Their condition varied from the almost new in Copenhagen Street to the single-bay sheds in a number of rural stations. Many were in need of refurbishment or literally tearing down, but money was not available in the years after the war. Among the more significant moves, the brigade identified the old railway storage buildings, (which now housed Waithnan and Cox furniture auctioneers) in Howsell Road to be their future home in Malvern and Brigade Headquarters moved from Bevere Manor to Copenhagen Street.

Communication in those days was mainly via the exchange telephone system. The method of alerting the retained personnel was by a combination of a call bell installed in the fireman's house and the 'all clear' tone of the former wartime air-raid sirens. Wireless communication equipment for appliances was some time off, but wireless cars for use by the officers were being introduced. The wireless facility had to be shared with the police.

The brigade fleet included twenty-seven light trailer pumps, twenty-five heavy trailer pumps, ten pump escapes, sixteen self-propelled appliances, sixteen towing vehicles, two turntable ladders, four salvage tenders, one breakdown lorry and one foam tender. Most of these machines were NFS-supplied with the rest from the pre-war services. Conversion work commenced on four towing vehicles, taking the trailer pumps and mounting them onto the chassis. Others were converted into a petrol carrier and salvage tender. Bromsgrove bought sixty-seven hydrants from the City of Birmingham Water Authority for £360, having previously rented them.

The major outbreak of the year occurred on 23 October 1948, when the Boughton Golf Club in Worcester was nearly destroyed by fire. Two major pumps from Worcester were joined by PE and ATV from Malvern and Ben Hitchcock and his men from Pershore.

Calls for the year April 1948-March 1949 totalled 1,004 including seven fatalities.

Conversion work continues on old NFS appliances like this Bedford at Kidderminster. Other appliances included an ex-army Fordson 7V WOT chassis, converted into a Stack Grab for tearing apart haystacks. C. Wooldridge collection

1949-1950

The brigade were experiencing a steady increase in the number of Special Service Calls. These are non-fire related incidents, for example road accidents. The special rescue and cutting equipment we have today could only have been dreamed of then, when the order of the day was hacksaws, crowbars and elbow grease.

Recruit training was done mainly at the Birmingham Fire and Ambulance Service Training School in Lancaster Circus, Birmingham.

The major fire of the year occurred at 1.52 a.m. on 21 February 1950 in Cowl Street, Evesham. A fire in a three-storey dwelling used as a lodging house quickly developed and turned into a 'persons reported' incident. Multiple rescues were carried out and a couple of occupants jumped. A couple of people sustained severe burns and two occupants suffered fatal burns.

Four major pumps were used, plus one MP (Warwickshire), one PE and one WRT.

Calls for the year April 1949–March 1950 totalled 1,652 including ten fatalities.

The opening of the Howsell Road Fire Station in Malvern on 14 December 1950 with Worcester's machines. Worcester City and County Fire Brigade archive

1950-1951

The new fire station at Howsell Road in Malvern was opened and the new front-line machines from Worcester were sent across for the grand opening. EFK 151, a beautiful Dennis F7 pump escape, and Commer QX pumps EFK63 and EFK622 were the first machines delivered post-war.

Hydrant conversion to the standard 2.5-inch round thread outlet pattern and new installations continued at a steady rate. Wireless equipment was starting to be fitted to all the new machines and some of the major pumping appliances. Another wartime machine was converted in workshops, bringing the total to five.

A distressing incident occurred on 21 March 1951 at Clent Villa Farm, Lutley. The brigade were called to a caravan fire where two children aged two and three died of asphyxia.

Special Service Calls were up again, with two aircraft crashes causing fatalities. The first happened near the River Teme, Bransford on 21 December 1950, killing the pilot. The second happened on 24 January 1951 at Manor Farm, Honeybourne, when a RAF plane crashed, killing two pilots. RAF crash tenders from Honeybourne attended, along with appliances from Evesham and Pebworth.

Calls for the year April 1950-March 1951 totalled 1,363 including seven fatalities.

The Commer QX water tender built by Carmichael and Son of Worcester was the first chassis chosen by the new brigade. EFK63 was commissioned in 1950 and was put on the run at Worcester. The appliance has stood the test of time and over fifty years later is still in existence. Worcester City and County Fire Brigade archive

The first arrival of the new Leyland Comet pump water tenders with 500Gpm pump and 400 gallon tanks. Ron Henderson collection

1951-1952

On 7 December 1951, following a call for assistance from the Bristol Fire Brigade, two pumps were dispatched from Kidderminster and Worcester under the command of a station officer, to assist in a massive oil fire at Avonmouth Docks, Bristol. The crews stayed and rendered assistance for upwards of sixty hours.

An explosion followed by a severe fire occurred at Albright and Wilson Ltd, Trinity Street, Oldbury at 1.39 p.m. on 10 July 1951. Two employees were killed in the explosion, which caused extensive damage.

The brigade were inspected in October 1951 by HM Inspector, Mr F. Dann OBE, who expressed satisfaction with all he had seen.

A Leyland Comet pump was delivered to the brigade, and three additional machines were put on order. In addition a new concept machine was on order which could see the demise of the pump escape. The age of some of the front-line appliances was causing concern.

Calls for the year April 1951–March 1952 totalled 1,378 including six fatalities.

The fledgling Worcester City and County Fire Brigade relied heavily on pre-war appliances like the Tenbury UDC Leyland FK6 CAB650, which served well into the 1960s. This photograph shows her sporting the new crest just by the driver's seat. Ron Henderson collection

1952-1953

An additional three Leyland Comet pumps were delivered to the brigade, improving cover and also causing a rationalisation of the fleet.

On 1 July 1952 the brigade were called to a fire in the Petroleum Storage Depot in Stourport after workmen had caused an explosion while using oxyacetylene torches. Foam and jets were put to good use in bringing the fire under control.

On Sunday 2 November 1952 a large-scale exercise was held in the Oldbury area, in which all available appliances took part, manned by full-time, retained and AFS crews. Exercise 'Grand Slam' lasted for nine hours and incidents were staged to test the brigade under 'atomic warfare' conditions. Appliances from the brigade also travelled over to help in the East Coast floods disaster of early 1953.

Calls for the year April 1952-March 1953 totalled 1,892 including three fatalities.

1953-1954

One of the main causes of fires during this period of heavy coal consumption was chimney fires, mainly because of a lack of regular sweeping. WC&CFB had long been campaigning for action to be taken against people who it could be proved had acted negligently. Under the Town Police Clauses Act 1847 these people could have a charge made against them.

Another of the new tasks facing the WC&CFB was fire inspections of hospitals, institutions, schools and industrial premises, of which 1,890 were carried out in the year. They were required under the Factory Act 1937, the Public Health Act 1936, the Petroleum Consolidation Act 1923, the Theatres Act 1937, the Cinematograph Act 1909 and the Fire Services Act 1947 and premises were to be visited on a regular basis.

The Bedford S composite appliance, FFK549, was delivered. Otherwise termed a pump water tender, it came supplied with a 45ft ladder, which replaced the old 50ft escape. The appliance was fitted with a 400 gallon water tank and a foam proportioner which gave an output of 2,400 gallons of foam per minute.

Another new addition to the fleet was a personnel carrier. This allowed the retained machine to turn out immediately with additional crew travelling in the PC.

On 11 May 1953 the brigade were called to Lumbertree Farm, Welland, near Malvern, to 'a man collapsed down a well'. On arrival they found one man had been rescued by the public, but another was still down at the bottom. Using improvised ladders and lines, two members descended and with the assistance of the police removed the other casualty to the surface. Carbon monoxide poisoning was found to be the cause of the incident. One member of the public was awarded the BEM and Sub Officer Jakeman received a Queen's Commendation for Brave Conduct.

Calls for the year April 1953-March 1954 totalled 1,524 including five fatalities.

The brand new Bedford S composite appliance delivered to Worcester, posed by the River Severn in 1953. Worcester City and County Fire Brigade archive

The first diesel appliance delivered to the Worcester City and County Fire Brigade was this Dodge Kew pump water tender for Kidderminster. Ian Scott collection

1954-1955

Two large fires occurred during the year, one on 2 June 1954 at Heenan Froude Ltd, Shrub Hill, Worcester where the roof caught fire causing considerable damage. On 26 June 1954 another large factory, John Garrington and Sons Ltd of Aston Fields, Bromsgrove, had a large outbreak causing damage to the heat treatment department and spraying rooms.

In March of 1955 exceptional weather conditions caused the brigade to attend an unusually high number of grass fires (seventy-six) and Special Service Calls. During the floods which followed, among the 107 pump-out incidents, a bus had to be towed to safety and the passengers rescued.

A rural firefighting party of seven members had been formed at the factory of W. Lusty and Sons Ltd of Martley.

A Dodge Kew composite pump was delivered to Kidderminster. This had a Hathaway 500psi pump. A Dennis F8 with a Metz 560psi pump was delivered to Worcester. Water savings were obvious and less water damage was the result.

Calls for the year April 1954-March 1955 totalled 1,792 including five fatalities.

Top: *The Dodge Kew HFK130 demonstrating the hose reel and the 45ft Ajax ladder on the sliding carriage at Worcester Station shortly after delivery.* Worcester City and County Fire Brigade archive

Above: *The brand new Dennis F8 pump water tender JFK670 was delivered to Worcester Station in 1953. This appliance was unique to the brigade in that it was fitted with a Metz 560Gpm pump.* Ian Moore collection

Hose Reel Equipment

Pre-war, the useful nature of hose reel equipment had been accepted and recognised as very much part of the fireman's armour. Now, nationally, there was general opinion that further development was required, the object being to reduce possible water damage, conserve water and also provide the capability of containing small petrol, oil and flammable liquid fires. Initial developments resulted in the production of a dual-purpose branch pipe which could produce either a small jet or a fog pattern spray. Owing to the fine mesh filters required to prevent the fog nozzle from becoming blocked, there was severe pressure loss. The equipment therefore was not particularly successful.

This led to attention being focused on the pump. The rotary hose reel pump did not attain pressures above 150psi. Attention was drawn to the specialist pump manufacturer, Hathaway, who had succeeded in producing a small centrifugal pump capable of delivering a relatively small quantity of water at high pressure (nominally 300-400psi.)

With a high-pressure pump installed into a fire appliance, initial trials proved very successful. With the additional development of a combined jet/spray pattern branch, the high-pressure hose reel equipment soon became very much part of the specification of the design for delivery of all new appliances. This in turn prompted manufacturers of large-scale fire pumps to examine their products, and it was not

The hose reel is very well demonstrated in this photograph of the newly delivered Bedford S Wilsdon-bodied appliance KFK308 at Worcester in 1956. Also of note is the 45ft Merryweather ladder on its sliding carriage. Worcester City and County Fire Brigade archive

long before an altogether new series of dual purpose high/low pressure pumps were produced, thereby allowing a single unit to satisfactorily perform both functions. Rotary hose reel pumps had now been relegated to history.

1955-1956

On 17 April 1955 the brigade were called to a 'van backed into a well of a disused gas holder' at the Gas Works, Oldbury. The well was 25ft deep and held in the region of one million gallons of water. The process of pumping out the water took time and a fireman from Oldbury, Fireman Elsdon, dived in numerous times to attempt rescues to no avail. For his actions he received a Queen's Commendation for Brave Conduct.

A large outbreak occurred at the National Tube Company Ltd, Halesowen on 8 September 1955. A large single-storey section of the factory was found to be well alight. Along with the firm's own fire section, WC&CFB appliances brought the blaze under control.

Road traffic accidents accounted for three deaths during 1955; two people were burned to death in an accident on 24 December 1955 caused by a defective petrol pipe; and in a separate incident on 29 July 1955, a lorry driver trapped in his cab on Eastham Bridge, Tenbury Wells died from multiple injuries.

One of the risks in a rural farming area is thatched roof fires. They are hellishly difficult to put out and very labour intensive. This one is at Charlton near Evesham and shows Commer EFK63 (Worcester) and Morris Commercial CAB992 (Pershore) tidying up after the fire had been extinguished. Worcester City and County Fire Brigade and Worcestershire Records Office

Composite appliances continued to be delivered with two Bedford S types arriving with Hathaway high-pressure pumps for Bromsgrove and Malvern.

Calls for the year April 1955-March 1956 totalled 2,249 including eight fatalities.

1956-1957

The major outbreak for the year was an incident at Regent Oil Company, Stourport-on-Severn, on 19 April 1956. The brigade were called at 8.42 p.m. to a petrol tanker on fire, believed to have been caused by a backfire from an adjacent tanker resulting in an ignition of petrol vapour during refilling. On arrival the WC&CFB found two tankers well alight under a collapsed corrugated iron filling bay carrying the supply pipes, with flowing burning spirit causing rapid fire spread to a single-storey garage measuring 200ft by 150ft and containing seventeen tankers which contained an additional 17,000 gallons of petrol. Immediate firefighting was concentrated on the high-exposure hazard of radiated heat to surrounding storage tanks, containing approximately two million gallons of petroleum products, and an office block.

Using fourteen jets from the river, street hydrants and foam branches from the composite appliances, 1,009 gallons of foam were applied to the fire. After two

Left and opposite: *The Regent Oil Fire in 1956 showing the vehicles destroyed in the inferno.*
C. Wooldridge collection

When Stourbridge Library caught fire in the late 1950s Dudley CB sent Leyland Beaver GXA83 (sister to Kidderminster's) to assist with the high-rise work. Worcester City and County Fire Brigade and Worcestershire Records Office

hours the brigade were able to contain the fire to the vicinity of the loading bay and the tankers, which were completely destroyed.

Civil Defence training exercises continued to be held across the area. Operation Redgrove, held at the Abbey Hostel, Redditch on 15 May 1955, was designed to demonstrate the effects in Worcestershire of a hydrogen bomb attack on the industrial part of the Midlands and the problems it would pose the various services.

Early and obsolete hydrants like the lamp column type were being replaced at an ever increasing rate. Hydrants available across the county numbered 8,334, with a further 420 awaiting acceptance.

Four appliances were delivered to WC&CFB in the period. One was a Dennis F8/Dennis, two were Dennis F8/Miles-bodied, Rolls Royce engined pump water tenders, with Hathaway high-pressure pumps and foam proportioners. One Bedford J2/Miles pump water tender, PFK108, was delivered to Redditch.

Calls for the year April 1956–March 1957 totalled 1,833 including five fatalities.

On 23 June 1957 at a fire in an Oldbury factory the local brigade were on the scene within four minutes. A single-storey building measuring 560ft by 700ft was found to be well alight, with the works brigade already fighting the fire with one jet. The WC&CFB set to work fighting the fire, and using thirteen jets from pumps and hydrants the fire was brought under control. The cost of replacing the 65,000sq ft factory was in excess of £250,000.

Special Service Calls were on the increase with a variety attended this year. Flooding pump-outs were also on the increase. Droitwich crews assisted at two serious RTA entrapments on 21 September, in which a car driver died in a collision with an HGV at Martin Husingtree. And on 24 September 1957, in another car collision with an HGV at Ombersley, a female driver was killed and two others seriously injured.

On 28 September a man was killed and three seriously injured, when a coach overturned at Wolverley, Kidderminster.

A call on 28 September to assist the police in apprehending a culprit on the roof of a building in Worcester brought the turntable ladder into action.

A twin-engined Miles Aerovan which was undertaking aerial photographic work crashed at Oldbury on 17 December 1957, killing the pilot. And to finish with, a man caught in a soda-crushing machine in a chemical works in Kidderminster on 4 February 1958 was released after a protracted rescue. He lost his leg, but not his life.

One Bedford J2/Miles pump water tender SFK500 was delivered to Kidderminster.

Calls for the year April 1957-March 1958 totalled 2,420 including two fatalities.

Broadway Fire Station opened in Keytes Lane in 1964 and was the same design as Pebworth's Station, which was opened in 1957, both being built by brigade personnel. Worcester City and County Fire Brigade archive

Assistant Chief Officer (ACO) Boutter, Assistant Divisional Officer (ADO) McCarthy and Station Officer (SO) Tidbury in front of men with the Worcester and Kidderminster turntable ladders pitched to the new tower at the official opening of the Halesowen Fire Station which was attended by many civic dignitaries. Worcester City and County Fire Brigade archive

1958-1959

New stations at Halesowen (above) and Pebworth (built by brigade personnel) were opened.

This was an appalling year for fire deaths, but one incident stood out above all others. In the early hours of 28 January 1959 the brigade were called to 'persons reported fire' at an address in Anchorfields, Kidderminster, which resulted in the deaths of a mother and her five children. The brigade arrived within three minutes to find a house well alight and members of the family still trapped. Two sets of BA and two jets brought the blaze under control. The cause of the fire, which severely damaged the property, was unknown, but a paraffin heater was involved in the fire.

Special Service Calls were again on the increase with a variety attended during the year. A serious RTA in Kidderminster on 21 June 1958, where a car collided with a building, resulted in three fatalities. On Fish Hill, Broadway on 3 October 1958, a van and a HGV collided and trapped three casualties who were released with multiple injuries. And on 18 February 1959 a lorry overturned near Stockton on Teme, trapping the driver by his legs. This was a protracted rescue involving oxyacetylene cutting gear and hydraulic jacks. The driver was released with severe injuries to his legs. The Superintendent of Kidderminster Police praised the brigade.

Two large AFS exercises were run during the year. Operation Wusterport was staged on 7-8 June 1958 at Newport Docks, Wales. It was designed to test the movement of a large column of appliances and to test equipment under competitive conditions. An inter-regional exercise, 'Eight-Nine', was held at Moreton-in-Marsh on 4-5 October 1958, involving twelve appliances manned by fifty-one personnel. It was organised to exercise personnel in fire operations of a mobile fire force, to practise reinforcement in the field and to provide practice in radio communications, map reading and driving in convoy.

Two Bedford J2/HCB, PWRT were delivered to Worcester and Stourport. One was fitted with a Coventry Climax high-pressure pump while the other had a Gwynne high and low-pressure pump.

Calls for the year April 1958-March 1959 totalled 2,091 including fifteen fatalities.

1959-1960

The whole United Kingdom Fire Service was shocked by the disaster at the Whiskey Bond Warehouse in Cheapside, Glasgow on 28 March 1960, in which nineteen members of the emergency services lost their lives.

The new Bewdley station became operational and replaced the cramped base in Guildhall/Townhall.

Repercussions for the future were identified with sixty-five men being awarded long service and good conduct medals. A lot joined during the war years and these

The new station at Bewdley, which replaced the previous cramped quarters. Worcester City and County Fire Brigade archive

would be leaving in a short period of time, which could cause recruitment problems and a sudden loss of experienced hands.

An unusual and tragic accident occurred on a cabin cruiser on the River Avon at Pershore on 28 June 1959. A twenty-year-old male was killed and three others injured when the mast struck a 66,000 volt high-tension cable. Falling sparks caused a severe fire on the deck.

During a particularly busy period between 4 and 10 July, 224 calls were dealt with of which ninety-five were received in the space of forty-four hours on 7 and 8 July 1959, due to the dry weather conditions.

On 5 September 1959 the WC&CFB were called to a fire at a chemical manufacturer in Oldbury. On arrival the brigade found a single-storey 60ft x 40ft premises with molten chemical (phosphorous) burning inside, with the works brigade trying to tackle the outbreak with sand. It was apparent that a serious situation was developing and additional assistance was requested. Using eight jets from pumps and five sets of BA the WC&CFB and works brigade confined the fire to seventy per cent of the building. The brigade had been in the building earlier dealing with a less serious outbreak.

On 31 October 1959 the brigade were called to the wool storage warehouse of Greatwich Ltd in New Road, Kidderminster. A large blaze was evident which the crews from Kidderminster, Stourport and Bewdley tackled using eight jets and TL (turntable ladder) monitor. Nearly 300,000lbs of wool was destroyed in the blaze which was started by a stray firework. A spate of farm fires in the Bromsgrove area in October 1959 resulted in a juvenile being apprehended and sent to court on charges of maliciously starting fires causing £6,000 damage.

Special Service Calls were on the increase with a variety attended this year. On 2 April 1959 the brigade were called to 'workman overcome by sewer gas' in a foul sewer shaft in Kempsey. On arrival, a workman was released using BA and given artificial respiration to good effect. The Local Authority commended the brigade. Acting on a call from the Ambulance Service on 3 July 1959, the brigade attended a call to a collision between two diesel rail cars near Kidderminster. In the course of the rescue 208 children and thirteen adults were assisted to safety.

During the severe storms of January and February 1960 the brigade dealt with 140 flooding and pump-out calls. The most serious incident of the period occurred on 3 February 1960, when high winds demolished a chimneystack weighing many tons, which brought down the roof of a pub in Worcester. A number of people were trapped and a passing female died from multiple injuries after being struck by debris. The brigade effected rescues and made the gas and electric supplies safe. The TL was employed removing dangerous brickwork.

Two large AFS exercises were run during the year. Exercise 'Spring' was held at Preston Docks during the weekend of 25-26 April 1959. A mobile column consisting of forty-three appliances, twelve motor cycles and 207 personnel from Worcestershire, Warwickshire, Staffordshire and Herefordshire were billeted for the night at the HO (Home Office) Training Centre, Chorley, Lancashire. The exercise was largely kept secret to increase realism, and was designed to underpin expertise in large-scale movements and fire ground operations in the event of a nuclear incident.

Regional exercise 'Quartette', held over the weekend of 27-28 June 1959 at the Fire Service Training Centre, Moreton-in-Marsh, involved a mobile column from No.9 Region, comprising ninety emergency appliances and 430 WT(wholetime),

Two Bedford 2/HCB, PWRT, have been delivered to Bewdley (above) and Pershore. By re-allocaton of appliances, two retained stations have now been equipped with self-propelled pumps and two ATV appliances can go for disposal. Worcester City and County Fire Brigade archive

Ret and AFS men and women from within the region. It was designed to cover the operation of a mobile fire force following a nuclear attack and Chief Officer Gerald Eastham acted as Mobile Fire Force Commander.

Hydrant systems continued to come on-line in many of the outlying parishes, and the completion of these schemes would double the number of hydrants that existed in 1948. Replacement of a further twelve ball-type hydrants in Droitwich and nineteen lamp-column-type in Malvern reduced the number still in operation to fifty-seven and sixty-one respectively. However, a great many areas still did not have a piped water supply for firefighting.

Calls for the year April 1959–March 1960 totalled 3,848 including three fatalities.

1960-1961

Another appalling year for fatal fires involving youngsters. Children playing with matches started a fire at Rous Lench on 17 July 1959, which destroyed a dutch barn and nearby property, and injured a retained fireman. Matches also played a part in a number of deaths starting on 4 April 1960, when two youths experimenting with matches and gunpowder found it a fatal combination, with one youth losing his life.

On 26 July 1960, in Blackheath, a couple of youngsters found matches and the resultant fire claimed a three-year-old's life. On 3 March 1961 children playing with matches dropped one into the tank of an abandoned car in Bromsgrove; the resultant explosion killed an eleven-year-old.

Right: *The Worcester Albion Mills fire at its height in the early hours of 11 December 1960.* Worcester City and County Fire Brigade archive

Below: *Being demonstrated on the Malvern Hills, Malvern's new Bedford R Series 4x4 pump with high-pressure hose jet.* Worcester City and County Fire Brigade archive

The major fire of the year occurred on 10-11 December 1960 in the old Albion Flour Mills in Mill Street, Worcester, a building of eight floors which was being refurbished into flats. A policeman on patrol spotted the fire and called the brigade at 11.05 p.m.

On arrival the OIC found that a serious fire had taken hold from floor five upwards, including the roof. Due to the sprinklers being switched off the fire had grown out of control. To prevent the fire spreading downwards, it was necessary for firemen to climb the vertical internal iron ladders, hauling lines of hose aloft to bring jets to bear. A total of nine jets and a TL monitor supplied by pumps working from hydrants and the canal to the rear of the premises were used. For reasons of safety forty families in neighbouring properties were evacuated. This was the largest blaze to hit the brigade since the war. Attendance: WRL (water ladder), WRT (water tender), TL (turntable ladder), PE (pump escape), PWRT (pump/water tender)-Worcester; WRL, WRT-Malvern.

A tragic Special Service call occurred on 23 October 1960, at Eckington on the River Avon. A cabin cruiser on a river trip with a young family on board stalled its engine and was dragged into partly open sluice gates where it capsized. Two young children were thrown overboard and drowned in the incident.

Two large AFS exercises were run during the year. Exercise 'Long Jump', held on 11-12 June 1960, was organised by Warwick CFB (County Fire Brigade) and held at Barry Docks, South Wales. It was designed to test the operation of a mobile column, including movement and procedure at a reinforcement base. Seven appliances, thirty personnel and two dispatch riders took part. Exercise 'Burtonwood', held on the 1-2 October 1960 at RAF Burtonwood, Lancashire, was organised by the WC&CFB. Fifty-one appliances, nine dispatch riders and 200 personnel from Worcestershire, Staffordshire, Wolverhampton, Herefordshire, Walsall, Birmingham, Smethwick and West Bromwich, and Shropshire attended the exercise.

The object was to operate a 'crash plan' including forming up a mobile column and organising feeding and sleeping arrangements, as well as practising movement of the column and emergency communications.

Two Bedford appliances were delivered during the year, one a Bedford J2/HCB, PWRT, to Halesowen, and a Bedford R Series, 800FFK, with 4x4 capability to Malvern.

Calls for the year April 1960-March 1961 totalled 2,620 including ten fatalities.

1961-1962

A number of major fires occurred in the region, starting on 27 May 1961 at a woodworking factory in Redditch. The factory was severely damaged and additional appliances had to come from Bromsgrove and Warwick CFB; the outbreak was controlled by eight jets and five sets of BA. An electronic equipment manufacturer in Lye was severely damaged on 20 September 1961, and additional assistance was requested before seven jets brought the fire under control.

Overleaf: *The Worcester PWRT Dennis F8 JFK670 has a number of lines run out at the Alley & Maclellans fire in 1962. The fire was fanned by strong winds which hampered operations.* Worcester City and County Fire Brigade archive

On 12 February 1962 the premises of Alley and Maclellans in Worcester suffered a fire which destroyed a factory unit and endangered a nearby CO_2 plant. Gale-force winds hampered operations, but with additional assistance using four jets the 'stop' was finally sent.

The major outbreak of the year though was at Midland Tar Distillers in Oldbury on 29 March 1962. On the scene in two minutes, the brigade found a horizontal tar oil tank containing about 8,000 gallons and the refined tar deck well alight, with flowing burning oil causing rapid spread to adjacent tanks, drums of tar and road and rail tankers.

The pipework of the complex and buildings in the vicinity were also at risk. The OIC immediately requested 'make pumps ten', which brought reinforcing pumps from WC&CFB and Tipton, Rowley Regis and Smethwick, and also the works brigades of Accles and Pollock, Tube Products and BIP Ltd. Crews faced extreme difficulties from dense smoke, heat, super-heated steam from fractured pipes and flowing molten tar, but their efforts succeeded in confining the fire in two hours to an area of 500ft x 500ft, and bringing it under control with twenty jets from hydrants and open water. Three firemen were injured in the blaze. Serious damage was caused to the tank farm comprising fifteen 8,000-15,000 gallon overhead storage tanks, 200 fifty-gallon drums containing road tar and associated loading gantries and pipework. A Leyland Octopus road tanker and a 2,200 gallon rail tanker were also destroyed. Associated buildings in the vicinity of the fire were also seriously damaged as photographs in the press the following day showed.

Special Service Calls were on the increase with the CFO stating his concerns over the trend of 'non-related fire calls'. A request to the brigade on 15 April 1961 to assist the police in a murder case they were working on involved pumping out approximately two million gallons of water from the Worcester to Birmingham canal to look for a weapon. Another incident involved a call on 4 August 1961 to an RTA involving a coach and two cars, to remove casualties trapped. Two youngsters of seventeen and nineteen were killed in the incident.

Calls for the year April 1961-March 1962 totaled 3,421 including nine fatalities

1962-1963

Death by misadventure was the verdict of the coroner in the case of a caravan fire on 17 February 1963 in which two young boys died in Redditch. The case was even more tragic when it was recalled that the two youngsters were rescued a year before from the same caravan after a fire.

An inquest determined that an explosion in a house in Hunnington on 6 September 1962, which killed a man, was caused deliberately while the man was in a disturbed state. Three people were rescued with burns.

On 9 April 1962 WC&CFB were called to IMI Summerfield, Kidderminster, to an explosion in one of the chemical manufacturer's research stations. The works brigade and two jets brought the blaze under control. Called to a fire at a tent and

Opposite: The aftermath of the major fire at Midland Tar Distillers in Oldbury on 29 March 1962. The devastated plant along with the burnt out remains of the Leyland Octopus tanker are submerged in solidified tar. Worcester City and County Fire Brigade archive

Two Bedford J2/Carmichael PWRT appliances were delivered to Oldbury and Redditch respectively. They were fitted with Gwynne dual-purpose pumps. A 45ft alloy ladder by Merryweather & Co was also purchased with a view to replacing the old 50ft escape ladders. Clearly seen in the bottom photograph is the new gantry for removing the 45ft Merryweather ladder speedily and which also greatly reduced the risk of back injury. Pip Potter collection

rope manufacturer in Tybridge Street, Worcester on 2 December 1962, the brigade found four four-storey buildings alight. Using a TL and eight jets, the brigade brought the fire under control and saved further fire spread. A fire which could have had the potential for large life loss occurred on 22 December 1962 when a bus was in collision with a motorcycle in Kidderminster. The motorcycle burst into flames which set the bus on fire; thirteen people escaped from the wreckage but the motorcyclist died in the incident.

There were 154 recorded Special Service Calls this year, the highest since WC&CFB came into being in 1948. RTA calls were increasing and the brigade were learning new skills in extrication. On 12 April 1963 at Hanbury, a trapped lorry driver was released by hydraulic rescue gear, but died from his injuries. On 19 April 1963, at Crown East, a motorcyclist was trapped under a bus following a RTA but was released using jacks and props, but he too died from his injuries.

On a lighter note, the TL from Kidderminster was called on 1 January 1963 to remove dangerous icicles from the viaduct. Also, chimney fires were at their highest

A new Morris FG/HCB was delivered to Worcester for conversion into Foam/Salvage Tender. Ian Moore collection

recorded level, with 1,020 incidents during the year. The message was reiterated to the public: it is your responsibility to keep chimneys swept.

Four junior firemen were appointed in July 1962. They undertook an eight-week physical training course with the local police force and in September they began a two-year programme of experience and training in all aspects of firefighting.

1963-1964

The most tragic event to happen during the year was the loss of Station Officer Kimberley of Worcester during an arduous rescue operation at Powick Hospital on 25 July 1963.

Two youngsters died from carbon monoxide poisoning in another caravan inferno on 21 January 1964 at Childswickham, near Evesham. The mother had just visited another caravan on the site and attempts by neighbours to rescue the youngsters proved unsuccessful. The major outbreak of the year occurred on 6 November 1963 at the Worcester Vinegar Works. Severe damage was caused to the roof and some areas of the factory. Although initially tackled by the works department, the WC&CFB, using five jets and a TL monitor, were needed to bring the fire under control.

Special Service Calls were on the increase with a variety attended this year. RTA incidents included a collision in Worcester on 1 April 1963 in which a female driver, who had been trapped in her van, died from multiple injuries. A triple-vehicle collision on 17 December 1963, on Fish Hill, Broadway, claimed the life of a lorry driver who was trapped in his cab. And finally, on 1 January 1964, a car which had crashed into a tree at Malvern claimed the lives of three youngsters. The brigade used axes, saws and crowbars to release the bodies and two others who were seriously injured. A workman died after he became trapped due to trench walls collapsing on him in Barnt Green on 16 July 1963. The brigade located and removed his body.

Out with the old, in with the new: Leyland TD7 is shown in its new role as a high-rise appliance with Rentokil Ltd. Ron Henderson collection

Bedford TK-Firefly Simon DS50, Kidderminster Station's new pump hydraulic platform. Ian Moore collection

On 26 December 1963 a new risk emerged when the WC&CFB attended the first major collision on the M5 due to fog. They were asked to wash away petrol and oil from the wrecked vehicles. A gentle introduction to the horrors to come!

Two large AFS exercises were run during the year. Exercise 'River' held at Preston Docks, Lancashire during the weekend of 24-25 August 1963 was used to test the movements of a mobile column. Ten appliances and eighty fire personnel were involved. Exercise 'Midst', held during the weekend of 21-22 September 1963, was designed to test the movement of the reserve vehicles and appliances to a supply base.

The replacement of obsolete hydrants continued and the number of operational hydrants stood at 10,174. The junior firemen ranks increased to seven and two sets of the 'Diktron' communication system, designed to be used in the facemasks of BA sets, were introduced.

A Bedford TK/Angus Firefly/Simon DS50 pump hydraulic platform went into operation at Kidderminster. 164YFK replaced the diesel-powered Leyland Beaver Turntable Ladder GXA63, which was transferred to Worcester to replace the petrol-driven Leyland TD7 turntable ladder GLW428, which went for disposal. Another Morris FG/HCB was delivered; 69XFK was stationed at Halesowen as a foam salvage tender.

Calls for the year April 1963-March 1964 totalled 2,870 including seven fatalities.

1964-1965

The new Redditch station on Birmingham Road was officially opened on 20 June 1964.

The major outbreak of the year occurred on the 24th August 1964, when a carelessly disposed cigarette caused a fire which destroyed the roof and second floor of the Lea & Perrins factory in Midland Road, Worcester. Fifty men, twelve appliances from Worcester, Droitwich, Malvern, Kidderminster, Bromsgrove, Pershore and Redditch and the Worcester TL and HLL (hose layer) fought the blaze throughout the night using fourteen jets from hydrants and open water.

Two smaller blazes required more than the initial attendance. On 9 July 1964 the brigade were called to a Stourport tannery, Henry Beakbane Ltd, and found the building well ablaze. Fifty-two men using nine appliances from Stourport, Kidderminster, Bewdley, Worcester and Droitwich (including the new PHP – pump hydraulic platform) and Worcester's TL, fought the fire and using twelve jets from hydrant and open water brought the blaze under control in two hours. On 28 November 1964 the brigade were called to a factory in Oldbury, to an outbreak believed to have started twelve hours before. Appliances from Oldbury and Halesowen were backed up by machines from Smethwick and West Bromwich, and using seven jets brought the blaze under control after about one hour.

Special Service Calls were at a record level of 206, the highest since 1948. The CFO stated: 'It is right that we should help when we can, when people have become trapped or at risk. Nevertheless it increases the workload at every level and requires special equipment to deal with the problem.' He was highlighting the problem that faced every chief across the country, that the only statutory duty of

'Vehicle checks', the start of every fireman's day. The machines parked at the back of the new Redditch station are a Leyland Cornet WRT, Bedford J2/Carmichael PWRT and Bedford EP. Worcester City and County Fire Brigade archive

The outbreak at the Lea & Perrins Sauce factory, Midland Road, Worcester, on 24 August 1964. Worcester City and County Fire Brigade archive

any brigade at that time was to fight fires, and who was going to fund the purchase of special equipment, vehicles and training that these new risks posed?

Two incidents stood out in the year. On 28 August 1964 assistance was given at the scene of an accident between a car and a goods train at a level crossing near Kidderminster. Of the five people in the car two were killed and three seriously injured.

On 1 December 1964 a driver joined the M5 going north on the southbound carriageway. There were a number of near accidents before he collided head on with another vehicle, resulting in two fatalities.

Manual telephone exchanges had been upgraded to incorporate automatic dialling which meant that most of the stations within WC&CFB could now be

The Control Unit used by the brigade was the Bedford SP, NYR824 which was stationed at Kidderminster then latterly at Droitwich. M. Lawmon collection

The new Bedford J4/HCB, PWRT stands resplendent in the sunshine at the Howsell Road station in Malvern. Worcester City and County Fire Brigade archive

called out directly from brigade control via the GPO DX callout system. Tenbury and Pebworth were among those to benefit.

The first intake of junior firemen had now been enrolled as operational firemen.

New hydraulic rescue kit had been purchased to assist in the ever-increasing rescue role.

Two Bedford J4/HCB, PWRT, had been delivered to Malvern and Kidderminster and the surplus water carrier at Worcester was disposed of.

Calls for the year April 1964–March 1965 totalled 3,548 including eleven fatalities.

1965-1966

A quieter year on the whole for the WC&CFB as incidents and deaths were down from previous years. A very wet summer was partly responsible. 'Bucket of water' primitive firefighting you might think, but that was all that was required to tackle a fatal fire incident in Droitwich on 27 January 1966. Smouldering clothes on top of a stove created enough smoke to asphyxiate a baby.

This was the first year in which there was no major outbreak in the area. There were a number of farm fires and factory incidents but most were dealt with by the initial attendance, and on only eight occasions were additional appliances required.

Malvern Station's off-road capability at cliff rescue incidents was provided by this Land Rover L4P, DVJ376C, which I photographed later in its career at Whitchurch.
Clive S. Shearman collection

Special Service Calls were the only area that remained at a similar level to the previous year at 205.

Cliff rescue was a particular skill which had to be mastered quickly in Malvern as the nine miles of hills and quarries were attracting ever increasing numbers of visitors. Three people were rescued in two separate incidents.

However, RTA incidents still provided the biggest test. On 17 August 1965 a car accident cost the lives of three people. On 8 November the brigade were called to an accident at Upton Warren, where a tanker had collided with a car. Firemen extracted four bodies from the wrecked vehicles.

The brigade now used only compressed air breathing apparatus sets. Also purchased were two sets of portable cutting saws operated from compressed air cylinders and one oxypropane cutting outfit for rescue operations.

Two Bedford J4/HCB, PWRT, were delivered to Bromsgrove and Stourbridge. Calls for the year April 1965–March 1966 totaled 2,797.

1966-1967

On 1 April 1966 Oldbury became part of the Borough of Warley. Bedford J2, 525NFK, which had served all its life at Oldbury, received the livery of its new master Warley Fire Brigade. This machine lasted through another change of name when in 1974 Oldbury became part of the West Midlands Fire Service.

The new premises of the Pershore Brigade in Defford Road officially became operational. The building was the former home of the Territorial Army in Pershore. Later in the 1960s the station also housed an ambulance for the Worcestershire Local Authority Ambulance Service. Worcester City and County Fire Brigade archive

Worcester's Leyland TL GXA63 gets to work at the front of J.C. Baker in Foregate Street on 2 June 1966. The supporting appliances are Worcester's Dennis F12 PE EFK151 and Bedford J2 pump 399SFK. Worcester City and County Fire Brigade archive

On 2 June 1966 the brigade were called to a spectacular fire which broke out at J.C. Baker, the ironmongers in Foregate Street, Worcester. Fire rapidly spread through the building and explosions were heard, which involved stocks of camping gas cylinders. The fire was brought under control using ten jets and a TL monitor. Crews from Droitwich and Malvern backed up the Worcester crews.

Severe damage was caused to Hindlip Police Headquarters on 18 October 1966. A delay was caused when occupants tried to fight the fire on their own using water/gas extinguishers and also tried to salvage documents. Appliances from Worcester, Bromsgrove, Droitwich and Kidderminster fought the blaze, using water from seven jets from hydrants, trailer pumps and open water. The TL from Worcester was used as a water tower. A relay of two pumps from a static water supply 400 yards away was also used.

Special Service Calls were slightly down for this year at 168. On 3 July 1966 Malvern firemen using lines had to rescue two youths attempting to climb a quarry face. And on the M5 at Droitwich a road tanker carrying concentrated sulphuric

Worcester's Bedford S PWRT FFK549 gets to work at the rear of J.C. Baker with the fire well established. Berrows Newspaper archive

acid overturned on 27 January 1967. The brigade stood by to dilute the spilt acid whist it was being transferred into carboys for disposal.

Her Majesty's Inspector of Fire Services, Mr A.V. Thomas OBE, GM, carried out the annual inspection of the brigade during November 1966. He replaced Mr F. Dann OBE, who had inspected the brigade since 1951.

Work commenced on the final stage of the centralisation programme to include Evesham, Upton-upon-Severn, Pershore, Broadway and Pebworth in the VF remote control system A. This was due to be completed in the next year when fourteen stations, WT, DM (day manning) and Retained could be directly alerted and mobilised from the control room at headquarters. A further eight sets of hydraulic rescue equipment were purchased, also quantities of high-visibility orange waistcoats for use at RTAs and inspections and yellow fireproof over trousers.

Three Bedford TKEL/Carmichael, PWRT, were delivered to Worcester, Redditch and Kidderminster respectively. These had the new 'Vista View' cabs.

Calls for the year April 1966–March 1967 totalled 2,382 including six fatalities.

Kidderminster's new Bedford TKEL Vista View, Carmichael PWRT. Pip Potter collection

1967-1968

The largest fire of the year occurred on 3 May 1967 as Kidderminster responded with two appliances to a fire at the British Sugar Corporation, Stourport Road, a sugar beet processing factory. On arrival the Officer in Charge found a severe fire had taken hold in a large single-storey warehouse containing 500 tons of refined sugar, stored in one-hundredweight paper sacks. Fire was rapidly spreading on the ground of the adjoining three-storey processing building and along two covered conveyors connecting large separate storage buildings. An immediate request for assistance brought additional pumps from Kidderminster, Stourport, Stourbridge and the hose-laying lorry from Halesowen. BA teams commenced a search for three maintenance engineers who were reported missing in the processing building. These men were quickly located and led to safety. Although the fire damage was considerable, the fire was quickly brought under control using eight jets from hydrants and a water relay from the canal, approximately half a mile distant. Six sets of BA were used. The fire was thought to have originated from sparks from welding equipment.

Calls for the year April 1967-March 1968 totalled 2,911 including five fatalities.

1968-1969

Two new stations were opened at Bromsgrove and Stourbridge replacing out-of-date, cramped quarters. The new Bromsgrove Station in Windsor Street also had a block alongside which were the quarters built for the firemen who would day-man the vehicle. The building now houses the Fire Prevention Department as the station has become full-time.

The Stourbridge Station may look unfamiliar with the appliances facing out of the rear of the station but when it opened the town was facing major road disruption and rebuilding so all turnouts were out of the rear of the station. This arrangement continued for months. Worcester City and County Fire Brigade archive

A number of serious outbreaks were reported during the year. On 17 July 1968 the brigade were called to a factory in Lye, where sparks in a large tyre-buffing machine had ignited rubber dust. Seven appliances and a hose layer brought the fire under control. On 13 December 1968 appliances from Stourbridge and Halesowen, including a FoT (foam tender), were called to an outbreak at a Lye chemical factory. Using four jets the fire was brought under control but the complex was severely damaged. And on 8 March 1969 the WC&CFB were called to a large fire which had taken hold at a Redditch tyre store. Using ten appliances and the new TL from Worcester, the fire was brought under control but 20,000 tyres were destroyed. Following a fire at the Shelton Mental Hospital in Shropshire, in which twenty-one patients were killed, an unprecedented level of requests for talks on fire safety and re-surveying of risks were received. On a lighter note, a bird which carried a lighted cigarette up to its nest was believed to have started a fire which destroyed the roof of a school.

Special Service Calls were at a record level of 239 with RTA calls continuing to be the main source of work. Releasing casualties trapped in vehicles was the main requirement with forty-seven cases of the brigade being called. On 9 August 1968 all these skills were called into use as a forty-one seat coach containing twenty-one passengers overturned and rolled down the embankment near Rashwood, Droitwich. Crews from Worcester and Droitwich assisted in extracting passengers to a fleet of ambulances. Seventeen people were injured with ten detained.

The first trials were taking place of so-called 'bleeper' mobilising for the retained staff. Callout for these staff had in the past been by the bell or the wartime siren.

A spectacular fire occurred at 6.55 a.m. on 7 December 1968, when a petrol tanker collided with a railway bridge at Spetchley and sheared the tank from the chassis. The load of 4,000 galllons of petroleum spirit was ignited by contact with the vehicle's exhaust and the fire quickly engulfed the railway embankment. Three appliances from Worcester, including the FoT and PWRT from Droitwich, brought the blaze under control using their foam-making generators. C. Wooldridge collection

The new AEC TGM/Merryweather 100ft turntable ladder outside Worcester Fire Station in 1969.
Ian Moore collection

Junior Firemen continued to be taken on with a further three being recruited.

A start had been made to adding 'Scotchlite' reflective strips to the RTA overalls purchased recently. Also purchased were eleven 120ft Terylene lowering lines for Malvern, and a Merryweather jet generator for the application of high expansion foam.

With thirty-six countries signing the Non-Proliferation of Nuclear Weapons Treaty, the immediate threat of nuclear attack had diminished. The Home Office decided to abandon the arm of the Civil Defence and the AFS and withdrew all 'Green' appliances to central storage depots. At the same time surplus vehicles were sold. WC&CFB decided to purchase the Control Unit NYR 824 (Kidderminster) and the hose-laying lorry equipped with 3.5-inch hose RYX 400 (Redditch), were added to the brigade fleet. Two Bedford TKEL/Carmichael, PWRT, were delivered to Stourbridge and Kidderminster. Also purchased was CFK291G, an AEC Mercury TGM-chassied, Merryweather 100ft turntable ladder for Worcester.

Calls for the year April 1968-March 1969 totalled 2,750 including one fatality.

1969-1970

Due to the very hot summer and dry period, grass fires reached a record level of 489. Two tragic accidents were the cause of fire deaths in the county. On 9 July 1969, the brigade were called to an RTA involving an HGV and a motorcycle in Redditch. A sixteen-year-old suffered extensive burns when his machine caught fire after the impact. And on 26 December 1969, a seventeen-year-old died after his car overturned and caught fire on the M5 at Rashwood, near Droitwich.

There were a total of 121 outbreaks within the region, but only on nine occasions were additional appliances required. The largest incident was in Stourbridge on

The new station at Merstow Green, Evesham opened in 1969. Worcester City and County Fire Brigade archive

Redditch's new Bedford TK/HCB Angus PWRT. M. Lawmon collection

Albion Reiver ex-petrol tanker, Bromsgrove. Worcester City and County Fire Brigade archive

16 December 1969, when the brigade were called to furniture manufacturers. Flames issuing from a damaged gas cylinder made firefighting difficult and stocks of foam plastic and timber bedheads assisted in the spread of the fire. Six appliances from Stourbridge, Halesowen and Kidderminster plus an additional appliance from Dudley brought the fire under control using six jets and a pump/HP.

Special Service Calls were at a record level of 287. RTA calls continued to be the main source of work. On 19 May 1969 appliances from Worcester and Pershore attended a collision between a HGV and car at Pershore. Two men received fatal injuries and on 4 September 1969 crews from Droitwich and Worcester were called to a HGV overturned at Droitwich. Heavy lifting equipment and hydraulic cutting gear were used in the protracted rescue, which saw two people cut free. One unfortunately was already deceased. Since February 1970, firemen at Pershore had been trying out the new personal 'alerter'. The alerting transmitter was linked to the remote control system (VF) used to mobilise the station from brigade control.

Two Bedford TKEL/HCB Angus, PWRT, were delivered to Redditch and Evesham. Also put into service at Bromsgrove was 342EYR, an Albion Reiver ex-petrol tanker which was converted into a 2,600 gallon water carrier for motorway and special risks.

Calls for the year April 1969-March 1970 totalled 3,303 including four fatalities.

1970-1971

A mother and daughter died in a house fire in Halesowen on 5 March 1971. On 19 July 1970 the brigade were called to a building previously used as a gaming club in Worcester. On arrival the crews found that an explosion had occurred and a severe fire was blazing. Three jets from the four appliances attending brought the blaze under control. After a search using BA a body was removed from the premises.

The largest outbreak of the year occurred on 1 August 1970 at the Perrywood, Metalbox site in Worcester. The factory containing paint, cardboard and timber caught fire and seven appliances using six jets and a TL brought the fire under control. The fire turned out to be of doubtful origin.

Two Bedford TKEL/HCB Angus, PWRT, were delivered to Stourport (above) and Bewdley.
Ian Moore collection

The brigade attended a tragic incident on 22 November 1970 when after putting out a fire in a Callow End cottage, four bodies were discovered and removed. A Coroner's inquest established that the occupier had killed his family and then taken his own life after setting fire to the premises.

Special Service Calls were at a record level of 315. A job at Kidderminster General Hospital, on 24 June 1970, utilised the new skills of line rescue. A workman was trapped after a collapse of scaffold 40ft in the air. Using a lowering line the workman was lowered to the ground but unfortunately his injuries proved fatal.

On 29 June 1970, following an RTA between a tanker and a car on the M5 motorway at Bromsgrove, the tanker started to leak its load of sulphuric acid. The brigade were called to neutralise the load using soda ash and by washing away.

Installation of the new PYE radio system had been completed. The scheme had two transmitters at Romsley and the other at Crowle. Additional sets had been provided for the salvage tenders and the station officers' cars, making the total number of sets purchased thirty-three. The personal alerters were proving a success and the siren system of callout was becoming a thing of the past. The Junior Fireman scheme had hit problems with no intake in the last two years. The main reason was sub-standard applicants.

Calls for the year April 1970-March 1971 totalled 3,321 including six fatalities.

1971-1972

The new station was opened at Stourport-on-Severn.

On 15 December 1971 a thirty-eight-year-old lorry driver received severe burns when his HGV crashed into a roadside filling station in Evesham. The fire, which severely damaged the building and a number of vehicles, was extinguished using three jets and four hose reels. The driver died in hospital as a result of his injuries.

On 30 April 1971 four appliances using water from three jets and three hose reels were required to extinguish a fire which broke out in a dormitory of a boarding school in Bushley. Two of the dormitories and the roof suffered severe damage. On 19 June 1971 the brigade were called to the BBC radio masts at Wychbold to fight a fire in the radio transmitting room. Firemen using BA found the oil-filled circuit breaker severely damaged by explosion and fire.

When a damaged motor coach pulled onto a garage forecourt in Holt Fleet on the 1 August 1971, nobody had any idea of the conflagration to follow. The heat of the exhaust ignited a fractured crankcase. The fire spread rapidly through the bus and to the forecourt buildings and petrol pumps. Pumps using three jets extinguished the blaze after a prolonged struggle.

On 1 November 1971, three appliances were called to a severe fire in Hanbury, in a single-storey pig shed with 100 tons of hay and hundreds of pigs. Using jets the fire was brought under control but 177 pigs were killed and the barn alongside was a total loss. On 3 November 1971, the brigade were called to a Bromsgrove furniture factory, where a severe fire was burning in one of the warehouses. Employees were forced to flee from the clouds of acrid fumes from the foam plastic used for upholstery. The fire was controlled by the operation of twenty-five sprinkler heads of the fully automated system. The brigade chipped in with two jets and BA. Two firemen were detained in hospital after being overcome by fumes.

A Dennis D/Dennis, PWRT, SFK400K, was delivered to Worcester, the first Dennis since NFK706 in 1956. M. Lawmon collection

Special Service Calls were at a record level of 354. An aircraft crash at Redditch on 12 June 1971 was attended by the brigade who assisted in the recovery of four bodies from the wreckage. Three incidents attended by the brigade involved leaking chemicals. On 2 June 1971 Kidderminster and Halesowen were called to deal with an incident in Kidderminster. Then there were two incidents on the M5, the first on 26 June at Strensham, where a tanker containing 100 gallons of hydrochloric acid overturned and started to leak. Worcester and Pershore crews dealt with the incident using soda ash. The second incident at Frankley Services on 29 October 1971 was more protracted and involved the chemical formaldehyde, which was leaking from drums on a HGV. Firemen using BA stood by while the lorry was unloaded and the chemical transferred to other containers.

Calls for the year April 1971–March 1972 totalled 3,249 including ten fatalities.

1972-1973

This was the end of an era with the retirement of Gerald Eastham as CFO. His replacement was Reginald Doyle, MIFireE, who was previously with City of Birmingham and Lancashire County Fire Brigades. (This appointment also included that of Chief Fire Officer [Designate] for the forthcoming combined Hereford and Worcester Fire Brigade. After a few years' service with this county, CFO Doyle moved on, being appointed as CFO of Kent Fire Brigade. He was latterly appointed to the Home Office [Fire Service Department] as Her Majesty's Chief Inspector of Fire Services.)

The biggest blazes of this year involved Dutch barns. The first, at Tenbury Wells on 13 September 1972, involved seven appliances from around the region.

The M5 RTA on 9 February 1973 near Bromsgrove shows the Albion Revier water carrier alongside Droitwich's PWRT. What is interesting to note is the introduction of rudimentary high visibility jerkins and the chevroning on the back of the Albion. Note also the M5 is still two lane and has no crash barrier. West Mercia Police Traffic Department

Approximately 300 tons of hay and straw were destroyed in the blaze and one of the main problems was water supply, as five appliances had to pump water over a distance of one mile to the incident. The second incident, on 21 October 1972, involved a six-bay barn in Upton-upon-Severn. Around 150 tons of hay were destroyed along with two tractors. Three appliances attended and using two jets from open water brought the fire under control.

A lorry on the M5 was severely damaged by fire on 9 February 1973 when heat from an electrical short circuit ignited polystyrene insulation on the tank containing over eleven tons of cooking fat. Appliances from Bromsgrove and Droitwich plus water carrier and foam tender attended and using jets and hose reels brought the fire under control.

Special Service Calls were at a record level of 364. Some things never change, with two children again having to be rescued from the quarry in Malvern.

The old wartime control room was demolished at Copenhagen Street in Worcester. Two Dennis D/Dennis, PWRT, XFK963K and XFK964K, were delivered to Malvern and Pershore.

Calls for the year April 1972-March 1973 totalled 3,712 including seven fatalities.

1973-1974

Two major fires occurred during the last year of the Worcester City and County Fire Brigade. On 9 March 1974 the first outbreak also involved the first operational deaths suffered by members of the brigade. The initial call to Hurcott Mill, Hurcott Lane, Kidderminster, indicated that a serious fire had taken hold in a large two-

Two Beford TK/HCB Angus, PWRT, TFK264M and TFK265M were delivered to Kidderminster and Bromsgrove. Ian Moore collection

storey building which was a former paper mill. The brigade responded with two appliances from Kidderminster. On arrival, the Officer in Charge immediately requested assistance. A total of ten appliances from Worcester, Stourport, Halesowen, Bewdley and Bromsgrove and the Worcester TL ended up fighting the blaze. While much of the building was unoccupied, the central parts were occupied by a manufacturer of upholstered furniture, having the associated risk of the storage of large quantities of polyurethane foam upholstery material. During protracted firefighting operations to contain the spread, a 'flashover' fire occurred within the loft where two firefighters equipped in breathing apparatus were operating a jet. Sub Officer Robert Crampin and Fireman Keith Marshall (Kidderminster), having been caught in the sudden unexpected inferno, were overcome in a mass of flame and lost their lives. A number of firemen were overcome by the dense smoke and fumes during the frantic attempt to rescue their colleagues and were conveyed to Kidderminster Hospital for treatment. Most were quickly released and returned to the fireground, although two members were kept in hospital overnight.

Two evenings later on 11 March 1974, and with little time to mourn the loss of their colleagues, the brigade were called to Pickfords Ltd in Sansome Street, Worcester. Two pumping appliances and the turntable ladder were dispatched. On arrival, the Officer in Charge was confronted with a severe fire involving the whole of a large three-storey building which was used as a furniture repository. The building was filled to capacity with household furniture and effects. To add to the difficulty of the task in hand, access for firefighting was restricted to two sides of the building. There was a severe risk of fire spread to adjoining and neighbouring property. As a precaution, the members of a clubroom were evacuated. The owners of an adjoining undertakers quickly arrived, and, on being appraised of the threat of

possible fire spread to their premises, made an urgent plea for assistance in the removal of bodies being kept in their chapel of rest.

The Officer in Charge made a request to control for additional appliances. Ten pumps from Worcester, Malvern, Pershore, Droitwich and Bromsgrove, together with the control unit and hydraulic platform from Kidderminster, were deployed at this incident. The fire was contained using six jets and the monitor from the TL supplied with water via pumps from street hydrants. Owing to the difficulty of extinguishing the deep-seated pockets of fire within the dense storage, relief crews were in attendance for some forty-eight hours.

At the time of writing, the outer walls of the building have been pulled down and the land cleared for rebuilding, some twenty-seven years after the fire occurred. It is understood that a recent planning application has been submitted to the Local Authority for the possible future development of the site.

Opposite and above. *Worcester Station's AEC Merryweather turntable ladder acts as a water tower as the first crews gain access at the height of the blaze at Pickford's warehouse in Sansome Street, Worcester, on 11 March 1974.* Worcester City and County Fire Brigade and Berrows Newspapers

I think this is a particularly fitting photograph for the end of this particular history book. It shows the wartime Leyland Beaver turntable ladder awaiting disposal. The crest of the Worcester City and County Fire Brigade is painted out as she awaits her next owner. This was the same fate that awaited the brigade in 1974; they need not have worried as Reginald Doyle took them forward to new heights.
Alan Davies

Opposite above: *Bedford TK/Firefly/Simon DS50, PHP, once transferred to the new Hereford and Worcester Fire Brigade.* M. Lawmon collection

Opposite below: *Bedford J2/Carmichael awaiting delivery at 'The Butts' in Worcester which was Carmichaels main site in the 1960s.* Pip Potter collection

Preceding pages:

During 1963 the Worcester City and County Fire Brigade sought tenders to replace the Leyland Beaver-Merryweather turntable ladder at Kidderminster. They had a number of tenders including Simon Platforms of West Bromwich. The particular demonstrator that was sent was on a Bedford TK chassis with 65ft booms. The pictures show the continuing tradition of appliances being tested at South Quay on the River Severn with the backdrop of the long since demolished power station which was one of the City of Worcester's major risks. Another item of interest about this appliance is that once it finished its life as a demonstrator it was sold to the Leningrad Fire Brigade in Russia. Worcester City and County Fire Brigade archive

Opposite:

Also at South Quay, firemen evaluate a diesal portable pump in the 1960s. The old power station is visible in the background. Worcester City and County Fire Brigade archive

Appendix

Fire Force 23 – Worcestershire – National Fire Service

FS No	LOCATION	PE	TL	M	LT	MDU 1000Gpm	OTHERS
A1							
A1Z	**Worcester FS,** A Division HQ *Copenhagen Street*	1	1	2	2	1	1 Control Unit 1 Emergency Tender 1 Fire Boat 1 Foam Tender
A1Z (a)	J. Archdale and Company *Blackpole Road, Worcester*			1	1		Alert Manning
A1Z (b)	Fire Force Headquarters *Bevere Manor, Worcester*			1			
A1Z (c)	Carr Retreat *Fernhill Heath*				1		1 Mobile Kitchen 1 Foam Tender Alert Manning
A1Z (d)	Worcester Royal Infirmary *Castle Street, Worcester*				1		Alert Manning
A1Z (e)	Russell and Dorrell Ltd *High Street, Worcester*				1		Alert Manning
A1Y	Pitmaston School *Pitmaston Road, Worcester*			4	4	1	1 Hose Layer 2 Pipe Lorries 1 Ramp Lorry
A1Y (a)	Alley and Maclellan Ltd *Bromyard Road, Worcester*				2		Alert Manning
A1Y (b)	Mining Engineering Company *Worcester*				1		Alert Manning
A1X	London Road *Worcester*			3	2	1	
A1X (a)	Worcester Royal Porcelain *Worcester*			1	1		Alert Manning
A1X (b)	Queens Head Public House *Kempsey*				1		
A1W	**Droitwich FS** *Friar Street*			2	3		
A1V	**Tenbury FS** *Teme Street*			1	1		MDU 500Gpm
A1V (a)	The Post Office *Newnham Bridge*				1		
A1U	**Malvern FS,** *Abbey Hotel, Great Malvern*	1		4	2	1	
A1U (a)	Victoria Road *Malvern*				1		
A1U (d)	Council Yard *Grundys Lane, Malvern*				1		
A1U (b)	Brookhouse *Colwall*				1		
A1U (e)	Council Yard *Merton Road, Colwall*				1		
A1T	**Evesham FS** *Vine Street*			1	1		MDU 500Gpm
A1T (a)	Victoria Arms Public House *Bretforton*				1		
A1T (b)	Steward Brothers *Broadway*			1		1	
A1T (c)	Lansdowne *Bengeworth*				1		Alert Manning
A1T (d)	Manor House *Fladbury*				1		
A1T (e)	Caravan Works *Harvington Cross*				1		
A1T (f)	Court Lodge *Cropthorne*				1		
A1T (g)	Bulls Head Hotel *Inkberrow*				1		
A1T (h)	School Road *Hampton, Evesham*				1		
A1T (j)	Long Hyde *South Littleton*				1		
A1T (k)	Badsey Lane *Badsey*				1		

NFS No	LOCATION	PE	TL	M	LT	MDU 1000Gpm	OTHERS
A1S	**Pershore FS** *Bridge Street*			1			
A1S (a)	Elmley Castle				1		
A1R	**Upton-upon-Severn FS** *New Street*			2	2	1	

B1

NFS No	LOCATION	PE	TL	M	LT	MDU 1000Gpm	OTHERS
B1Y	**Pebworth FS** *Station Lane*				1		
	C Division and C1 Sub Division combined						
	Wollescote Hall, Lye, Near Stourbridge						

C1

NFS No	LOCATION	PE	TL	M	LT	MDU 1000Gpm	OTHERS
C1Z	**Stourbridge FS** *Smithfield*	1		1	2		
C1Y	Amblecote *Stourbridge*			2	7		
C1X	**Lye FS** *Hill Road*			2	6	1	
C1W	Halesowen *Mucklows Hill*	1		3	7	1	
C1V	Cornbow *Halesowen*			3	4		MDU *500Gpm*
C1V (a)	The Elms *Colley Lane, Cradley Heath*			2			
C1U	**Halesowen FS** *Hayley Green*			2	3	1	*1 Pipe Lorry*
C1T	**Kidderminster FS** *Castle Road*	1	1	1	7		*1 Canteen Van*
C1T (a)	Mill Street *Kidderminster*			4	2	1	*1 Hose-laying Lorry*
							1 Canteen Van
							1 Foam Tender
							1 Ramp Lorry
C1T (b)	**Bewdley FS** *Load Street*			3	3		
C1T (c)	The Stables, Brackencote Hall *Chaddesley Corbett*				1		
C1T (d)	Steel Stampings Ltd *Cookley*				1		
C1T (e)	Original Stores *Rock*				1		Alert Manning
C1S	**Stourport FS** *Mitton Street*			3	6	3	*1 Fire Boat*
							1 Foam Tender
C1S(a)	William Allday & Company Alcosa Works *Stourport*				1		

C2

NFS No	LOCATION	PE	TL	M	LT	MDU 1000Gpm	OTHERS
C2	**Redditch FS** *Red Lion Street*	1		2	6	1	*1 Hose-laying Lorry*
							1 Foam Tender
							1 Hose Carrier
							1 Pipe Lorry
C2Z (a)	Manor House *Astwood Bank, Redditch*			1			
C2Z(b)	Swan Hotel High Street *Studley*			1	1		
C2Z(c)	Ideal Garage *Hopwood, Redditch*				1		
C2Y	Redditch *Birmingham Road*			3	5	1	
C2X	**Bromsgrove FS** *Churchfields*	1		3	5	1	*1 Emergency Tender*
C2X(a)	Leach Heath Lane *Rubery*			1	2		
C2X(b)	Nash Forge *Belbroughton*				2		
C2X(c)	Wynsford *Twatling Road, Barnt Green*				1		

Pre-war Worcestershire and Worcester City & County Fire Brigade

Fire Stations

TOWN		NFS	1948	1974	ORIGINAL BRIGADE/SERVICE	OPEN	CLOSE
Bewdley	Guildhall	C1T(b)			Bewdley MB – *NFS*	1800s	1948
	Guildhall		14		Worcester City & County		1960
	Load Street, Dog Lane		14		Worcester City & County	1960	1974
	Load Street, Dog Lane			23	**Hereford & Worcester FB**		
Blockley	Sheep Street – *Station Closed*				Blockley RDC		1931
Broadway	Keytes Lane				Broadway Volunteer FB	1897	1933
	Keytes Lane	A1T(b)			Evesham & Pershore RDC&JFB – *NFS*	1933	1948
	Keytes Lane – 1952		l0B		Worcester City & County	1964	1974
	Keytes Lane			30	**Hereford & Worcester FB**		
Bromsgrove	The Strand				Bromsgrove Volunteers	?	1879
	St John Street				Bromsgrove Volunteers	1879	
	Churchfields	C2X			Bromsgrove UDC – *NFS*	?	1948
	Windsor Street		6		Worcester City & County	1969	1974
	Windsor Street			25	**Hereford & Worcester FB**		
Clifton on Teme	Vicarage yard – *Station Closed*				**Worcester City & CFB** – *NFS*		1950s
Droitwich	Friar Street	AlW			Droitwich Borough & RDC – *NFS*	1892	1948
	Friar Street		8		Worcester City & County		1974
Droitwich Spa	Friar Street			26	**Hereford & Worcester FB**	1981	
Evesham	Vine Street				Evesham Borough	1887	1933
	Vine Street	AlT	10		Evesham & Pershore RDC&JFB – *NFS*	1933	1948
	Vine Street		10	28	Worcester City & County – H&WFB	1965	1974
	Merstow Green			28	**Hereford & Worcester FB**		
Halesowen	Great Cornbow	CIV			Halesowen MB – *NFS*	1800s	1948
	Great Cornbow		5		Worcester City & County		1957
	Hayley Green		5		Worcester City & County	1957	1974
	Hagley Road			F4	**West Midlands FS**		
Inkberrow – *Station Closed*					**Worcester City & CFB** – *NFS*		1950s
Kidderminster	Vicar Street				Kidderminster Borough Council		1929
	Castle Road	CIT			Kidderminster Borough Council – *NFS*	1929	1948
	Castle Road – 1955	2			Worcester City & County		1974
	Castle Road – 1987			24	**Hereford & Worcester FB**		
Lye	Hill Road – *Station Closed*				Lye & Wollescote – Stourbridge MC	1909	1948
Malvern	Victoria Road	A1U(a)			Malvern UDC – *NFS*	1890	1948
	Victoria Road – *Station Closed*	12A			Worcester City & County	1947	1948
Malvern Link	Pickersleigh Road	A1U			Malvern UDC – *NFS*	1940s	1948
Malvern	Lower Howsell Road		12		Worcester City & County	1950	
				41	Worcester City & County – H&WFB		1974
	Worcester Road			41	**Hereford & Worcester FB**	1983	

TOWN		NFS	1948	1974	ORIGINAL BRIGADE / SERVICE	OPEN	CLOSE
Malvern Wells	Grundys Lane	AlU(d)			Malvern UDC – *NFS*	1897	
	Grundys Lane – *Station closed*12B				Worcester City & County		1948
Oldbury	Tower Street				Oldbury MB – *NFS*	1889	1948
	Tower Street				Worcester City & CFB		1966
	Perrot Street				Warley CB	1968	1974
				D01	**West Midlands FS**		
Pebworth	Station Lane	B1Y(f)			Pebworth RDC – *NFS* Worcester		1948
	Broadmarston		10A		City & County	1959	1974
	Broadmarston			29	**Hereford & Worcester FB**	1959	
Pershore	Church Street				Pershore RDC	1885	1905
	Bridge Street				Pershore RDC	1905	1933
	Bridge Street	A1S			Evesham & Pershore RDC&JFB – *NFS*		1948
	Bridge Street		9		Worcester City & County	1966	1974
	Defford Road			31	**Hereford & Worcester FB**		
Redditch	Easemore Lane				Redditch Volunteer FB	1841	1881
	Alcester Street/Park Road				Redditch Volunteer FB	1881	1933
	Red Lion Street	C2			Redditch RDC – *NFS*	1933	1948
	Red Lion Street		7		Worcester City & County		1964
	Birmingham Road		7		Worcester City & County	1964	1974
				27	**Hereford & Worcester FB**		
Stourbridge	Market Street				Stourbridge Volunteer FB	1879	1888
	Corn Exchange, New Street				Stourbridge Volunteer FB	1888	1926
	Smithfleid	C1Z			Stourbridge MC – *NFS*	1926	1948
			3		Worcester City & County		1968
	Parkfield Rd		3		Worcester City & County	1968	1974
				D05	**West Midlands FS**		
Stourport-on-Severn	The Rickyard				Stourport Volunteer FB	?	?
	Mitton Street				Stourport UDC		1935
		C1S			Stourport UDC – *NFS*	1935	1948
	Mitton Street		15		Worcester City & County		1971
	Foundry Street		15		Worcester City & County	1971	1974
				22	**Hereford & Worcester FB**		
Tenbury Wells	Church Street				Tenbury RDC	1858	1938
	Teme Street	A1V			Tenbury RDC – *NFS*	1938	1948
	Teme Street		13		Worcester City & County		1974
				53	**Hereford & Worcester FB**		1988
	Worcester Road			53	**Hereford & Worcester FB**	1988	
Upton-upon-Severn	New Street				Upton-upon-Severn RDC	?	?
	New Street	A1R			Upton-upon-Severn RDC – *NFS*	1939	1948
			11		Worcester City & County		1974
				32	**Hereford & Worcester FB**		1991
	Minge Lane			32	**Hereford & Worcester FB**	1991	
Worcester	Copenhagen Street				Worcester City Police Fire Brigade	?	1941
	Copenhagen Street	A1Z			*NFS*	1942	1948
			I		Worcester City & County		1974
				21	**Hereford & Worcester FB**		

Pre-war Worcestershire and Worcester City & County Fire Brigade

Pumping Appliances

Reg No	TYPE	Registration Date	OS	BRIGADE	DETAILS/STATIONS
					Allday & Onions
AB1419	Pump	14.11.1910	?	Oldbury UDC	Tower Street
					Bedford WLG Series
AMY433	Pump	1934		Bewdley Borough Council	Load Street – *Purchased secondhand, 1935*
			56	WC&CFB	14 Load Street
					Buick Six
?	Tender	?	41	Droitwich Borough & RDC	Friar Street
					Dennis N Series
?	Pump	1910	40	Redditch UDC	Park Road/Red Lion Street
?	Pump/E	1912	32	Malvern RDC	Victoria Road – named '*Lady Grey*'
?	Pump	1916	39	Stourbridge Volunteer FB	Market St, Smithfield – *named 'Douglas'*
AB9139	Pump	02.03.1921	47	Borough of Halesowen	Great Cornbow
NP3332	Pump	23.11.1923	42	Borough of Kidderminster	Castle Road/2 Kidderminster/R
NP4411	Pump	11.06.1924	50s	Borough of Evesham – WC&CFB	Vine Street/10 Evesham/R
					Dennis 'G' Series
UY6975	Pump	28.12.1929	?	Redditch UDC -WC&CFB	Red Lion Street/7 Redditch
					Dennis 'Ace' Series
WP7645	Pump	05.02.1935	55	Bromsgrove UDC-WC&C	Churchfields/6 Bromsgrove/R/P
BUY353	Pump	29.07.1937	59	Stourport-on-Severn UDC	Milton Street
				WC&CFB	15 Stourport/R
					Leyland FE1 Series
AB6647	Pump	15.12.1919	?	Bromsgrove UDC	Churchfields
AB7432	Pump/E	06.12.1919	?	Oldbury UDC	Tower Street – *receivced plate May 1920*
					Leyland FE2 Series
UY3478	Pump/E	07.06.1928	35	Bromsgrove UDC	Churchfields
					Leyland FKI Cub
WP2649	Pump	07.11.1932	62	Malvern UDC	Victoria Rd & Malvern Link
				WC&CFB	4 Oldbury/R Preserved
					Leyland FK6 Cub
AWP486	Pump/E	31.10.1936	60s	Oldbury UDC – WC&CFB	Tower Street
CAB650	Pump	06.04.1938	68	Tenbury Wells RDC – WC&C	13 Teme Street/Tenbury/63/R/P
					Leyland FK8 Cub
DAB407	Pump	22.06.1939	60s	Halesowen MB	Great Cornbow/Hayley Green
				WC&CFB	5 Halesowen/R
					Leyland FK9 'Tiger'
DNP72I	Pump/E	01.01.1940	69	Stourbridge MB	Smithfield-Stourbridge
				Worcester City & CFB	Churchfields-Bromsgrove-65
				Warley CB	Perrott St-Oldbury/R Preserved

Reg No	TYPE	Registration Date	OS	BRIGADE	DETAILS / STATIONS
					Leyland FK2 'Tiger'
DNP752	Pump/E	07.01.1940	69	Redditch UDC	Red Lion Street
				WC&CFB	7 Redditch-61/4 Oldbury/R/P
					Merryweather Fire King
FK201	Motorised Steamer	14.07.1905	24 33	Norwich Union Insurance Co	Angel Place Upton-upon-Severn
					Morris Commercial F
UY4032	Pump	08.09.1928	31	Blockley RDC North Cotswolds FB	Sheep Street
WP1293	Pump	07.01.1932	?	Lye & Wollescote UDC WC&CFB	Hill Road
					Morris Commercial FD
WP689	Pump	29.08.1931	48	Upton-upon-Severn RDC	New Street 6x4
					Morris Commercial C
FK6363		14.09.1934	57	Worcester City Police FB City of Worcester – WC&CFB	1 Worcester-50/14 Bewdley/P *Bodywork – B.S. Brewer*
CAB992	Pump	18.05.1938	61	Evesham & Pershore RDC&JFB Worcester City &CFB	Bridge Street/Pershore-53 Reserve *photo at Bewdley*
					Morris 5cwt Minor
UY7858	Tender	17.04.1930	?	Oldbury UDC	Tower Street
					Napier
AB4404	Manual	19.06.1915	?	Borough of Kidderminster	Castle Road
					Panhard 30hp
AB6838	Tender	06.02.1920	32	Lye & Wollescote UDC	Hill Road
					Wolseley Siddeley
AB9532	Tender	02.05.1921	38	Evesham & Pershore JFB	Bridge Street/Pershore *Donated 1931*

Worcestershire and Worcester City & County Fire Brigade

National Fire Service Appliances

Reg No	TYPE	Registration Date	OS	BRIGADE	DETAILS / STATIONS	
						Austin K2
?	ATV	?			*National Fire Service*	Pebworth
GLE165	ATV	?	64		*National Fire Service*	Broadway
GLR93	ATV	41	61		*NationalFire Service*	Howsell Rd-Malvern
GLT655	ATV	?			*National Fire Service*	Copenhagen St-Worcester
GXH609	ATV	43	?		*National Fire Service*	Merton Rd/Howsell Rd, Malvern
GXH658?	ATV	43	?		*National Fire Service*	Castle Road-Kidderminster ?
						Austin K4
GXA765	ECU	43			*National Fire Service*	Oldbury
GXA780	P8397	ECU	43	64	*National Fire Service*	Malvern
GXM148	MDU	43			*National Fire Service*	Copenhagen Street, Worcester
						Bedford 'QL'
?	Pump				*National Fire Service*	Malvern – *proved unsafe/scrapped*
						Dodge 'Kew'
FYH???	Pump	40			*National Fire Service*	Broadway
GXM635	MDU	43			*National Fire Service*	Copenhagen Street, Worcester
						Fordson '7V'
?	Pump	40	62		*National Fire Service*	?/Upton-upon-Severn
?	Pump	?	57		*National Fire Service*	Droitwich
?	ECU	42	?		*National Fire Service*	Kidderminster
?	ECU	42			*National Fire Service*	Droitwich
?	ECU	42	52		*National Fire Service*	Castle Road-Kidderminster
GLD147	ECU	42	52		*National Fire Service*	Copenhagen Street-Worcester
						Morris Commercial
GMU191	Pipe/Layer				*National Fire Service*	Copenhagen Street-Worcester

Post war Worcestershire and Worcester City & County Fire Brigade

Pumping Appliances

During the period 1950-1970, many of the new pumping appliances received were allocated in the first instance to full-time or operationally busier stations for a short period of time. They were then subsequently allocated as the second appliance in the running order or allocated to the retained stations. This policy was adopted in order to obtain the best possible cost benefit during the service of the vehicle.

Reg No	Fleet No	TYPE	YR	OS	BRIGADE	DETAILS / STATIONS
						Bedford R Series
800FFK		WRT	61	82	Worcester C&C-H&WFB	12 Malvem-79/48 Eardisley-81-R 4x4
						Bedford S Series
FFK549		P/Wrt	53	72	Worcester City & CFB	1 Worcester-59/13 T Wells-69/R
KFK308		P/Wrt	55	72	Worcester City & CFB	1 Worcester/12 Malvern-69/R
KFK309		P/Wrt	55	78	Worcester C&C-H&WFB	6/25 Bromsgrove-74-76/R
						Bedford J2 Series
PFK108		P/Wrt	57	79	Worcester C&C-H&WFB	7 Redditch-62/8 Droitwich-69
						13/53 Tenbury Wells-78-R
SFK500		WRL	58	76	Worcester City & CFB	2 Kidderminster-65-R-76
					Hereford & Worcester FB	Sold to Guernsey
VFK600		WRT	59	?	Worcester C&C-H&WFB	15/22 Stourport-76-R
VFK60I		WRT	59	?	Worcester C&C-H&WFB	1 Worcester/10/28 Evesham-78-R
500AFK		WRT	60	78	Worcester C&C-H&WFB	14 Bewdley-62/
						11/32 U o Severn-76-R
501AFK		WRT	60	76	Worcester C&C-H&WFB	9 Pershore-72/7 Redditch-Retained
900FFK		P/Wrt/PL	61	78	Worcester CCFB-WMFS	10 Halesowen-72-R
525NFK		Wrt/P	62	78	WC&C-66-Warley -74-WM	4/E5/D1-Oldbuiy-76R
526NFK		WRT	62	79	Worcester C&C-H&WFB	7 Redditch-69/8/26 Droitwich-78-R
399SFK		Wrt/L	63	79	Worcester C&C-H&WFB	1/21 Worcester-Retained-78-R
400SFK		WRT	63	72	Worcester City & CFB	2 Kidderminster-67-R
401SFK		WRT	63	79	Worcester C&C-H&WFB	13/53 Tenbury Wells-79 Preserved
						Bedford J4 Series
EFK270C		WRT	65	81	Worcester C&C-H&WFB	12/41 Malvern/15/22 Stourport-80R
EFK271C		WRL	65	76	Worcester C&C-H&WFB	2 Kidderminster -R/Destroyed in fire
KFK945D		WRT	66	79	Worcester C&C-H&WFB	6 Bromsgrove-74/29 Pebworth-76T/P
KFK946D		Wrl/P	66	78	Worcester C&C-WMFS	3/F5/D5-Stourbridge-76-R Preserved
						Bedford TK-KEL-KE
TFK112E		WRT	67	82	Worcester C&C-H&WFB	1/21 Worcester/22 Stourport-81-R
TFK113E		WRT	67	80	Worcester C&C-H&WFB	7/27 Redditch-76/30 Broadway-80-R
TFK114E		Wrt/PL	67	79	Worcester C&C-WMFS	2 Kidderminster-71/F4/D4 Halesowen
YFK951G		Wrl/PL	68	82	Worcester C&C-WMFS	3/F5/D5 Stourbridge-76-Training
AFK369G		WRT	68	82	Worcester C&C-H&WFB	2/24 Kidderminster-80-T
					Dudley's Coach's	Derelict at Martley-Worcestershire
EFK108H		WRT	69	82	Worcester C&C-H&WFB	7 Redditch/6/25 Bromsgrove-81-T
EFK109H		WRT	69	82	Worcester C&C-H&WFB	10/28 Evesham-79/24 Kidderminster
LFK454J		WRL	70	83	Worcester C&C-H&WFB	2/24 K'minster-76/26 Droitwich-81-R
LFK455J		WRT	70	83	Worcester C&C-H&WFB	14 Bewdley-74/23 Bewdley-81-R
KFK584J		WRT	70	83	Worcester C&C-H&WFB	7 Redditch-74/27 Redditch-80-R
KFK585J		WRL	70	83	Worcester C&C-H&WFB	1/21 Worcester-76-R
SFK398K		WRT	71	83	Worcester C&C-H&WFB	15/22 Stourport-83-R

Reg No	Fleet No	TYPE	YR	OS	BRIGADE	DETAILS/STATIONS
SFK399K		Wrl/PL	71	82	Worcester C&C – WMFS	5/F4/D4 Halesowen-79-Training

Type B now fitted with the 6-cylinder Rolls Royce petrol engine

Reg No	Fleet No	TYPE	YR	OS	BRIGADE	DETAILS/STATIONS
TFK264M		WRL	74	85	Worcester C&C-H&WFB	2/24 Kidderminster-78-Reserve
TFK265M		WRT	74	84?	Worcester C&C-H&WFB	6/25 Bromsgrove-81-R
					Fordwater Pump Supplies	Lydney-Gloucestershire

Commer 21A & 45A Series – The 21A was used mainly for WRTs where the 45A was used for the heavier Pump/E and Pump/L.

Reg No	Fleet No	TYPE	YR	OS	BRIGADE	DETAILS/STATIONS
EFK63		WRT	50	70	Worcester City & CFB	1 Worcester-53/9 Pershore
						15 Stourport/13 Tenbury-R & P
EFK622		WRT	50	72	Worcester City & CFB	1 Worcester-53/11 U on Severn/R

Dennis Fl2 Series

Reg No	Fleet No	TYPE	YR	OS	BRIGADE	DETAILS/STATIONS
EFK151		Pump/E	51	75	Worcester CCFB-H&WFB	1/21 Copenhagen Street

Dennis F8 Series

Reg No	Fleet No	TYPE	YR	OS	BRIGADE	DETAILS/STATIONS
JFK670		P/Wrt	53	79	Worcester CCFB-H&WFB	1 Worcester-66/29 Pebworth-78-HGV
						Lying derelict at Samsung-Telford *Metz*
PFK272		P/Wrt	56	77	Worcester CCFB-H&WFB	8/28 Evesham-76-R
NFK705		P/Wrt	56	77	Worcester CCFB-H&WFB	12 Malvern/14 Bewdley
						10B/30 Broadway-76/R
					Newland Court Farm	Malvern, Worcestershire
NFK706		P/Wrt	56	72	Worcester City & CFB	2 Kidderminster-66/15 Stourport-R
						Lying derelict at Samsung-Telford

Dennis D Series – Type B now fitted with the 6-cylinder 4.2 Jaguar petrol engine

Reg No	Fleet No	TYPE	YR	OS	BRIGADE	DETAILS/STATIONS
SFK400K		Wrt/L	71	85	Worcester CCFB-H&WFB	1 Worcester-74 /21 Ret-RTA in 72
XFK963K		WRL	72	85	Worcester CCFB-H&WFB	12/41 Malvern-83-R
XFK964K		WRT	72	85	Worcester CCFB-H&W FB	9/31 Pershore-83-R

Dodge Kew Series

Reg No	Fleet No	TYPE	YR	OS	BRIGADE	DETAILS/STATIONS
HFK130		WRT	54	73	Worcester City & CFB	1 Worcester/2 Kidderminster

Leyland Comet

Reg No	Fleet No	TYPE	YR	OS	BRIGADE	DETAILS/STATIONS
FFK350		Pump	52	77	Worcester CCFB-WMFS	2 Kidderminster/5 Halesowen-71-R
FFK636		Pump	52	72	Worcester CCFB-1966	12 Malvern-61/4 Oldbury-66
					Warley CB	Perrott St-Oldbury-71-Reserve
FFK760		Pump	52	71	Worcester City & CFB	3 Smithfield-Stourbridge-69-Reserve
FFK820		Pump	52	74	Worcester City & CFB	7 Redditch-72-Reserve

Records show Leyland Comets serving at Droitwich, Pebworth, Stourport and Upton-upon-Severn

Post war Worcestershire and Worcester City & County Fire Brigade

Specialist Appliances

Reg No	Fleet No	TYPE	YR	OS	BRIGADE	DETAILS/STATIONS
						AEC Mercury TGM
CFK29IG		Turntable	68	91	Worcester City & CFB-H&WFB	Copenhagen St-74/21 Worcester-91
	MW-154	Ladder	91		Liverpool Docks	Merseyside
						Albion Reiver
342EYR		Water	63		Worcester City & County	ex -Petrol Tanker-2600 g W
		Carrier		79	Hereford & Worcester FB	Bromsgrove-74 /25 Bromsgrove-79
					Blenheim Palace	Oxfordshire – *used to water gardens*
						Austin K4
GXN23I	31	Turntable	44	64	Worcester City & County FB	E24 Castle Rd-Kidderminster
		Ladder				Preserved
						BEDFORD
164YFK		Pump	64	82	Worcester CCFB	Castle Rd-Kidderminster-74
		Hydraulic			Hereford & Worcester FB	24 Kidderminster
		Platform	82		National Exhibition Centre	Birmingham
						TKEL-Angus Fire Fly-Simon DS50
?		Stack Grab	45		Worcester City & County FB	*Fordson WOT-(War Office Type)*
NYR824		Control	55	81	Worcester City & County	cx AFS-68/#2/24 Castle Rd-
		Unit			Hereford & Worcester FB	Kidderminster
						SP-HOS
						BMC
425UFK		Foam	63	83	Worcester City & County	SDI Copenhagen St-74
		Salvage			Hereford & Worcester FB	21 Worcester-77
						Converted Foam/Salvage/ET
						21 Worcester-83 Damaged RTA-w/o
						Morris FG-HCB
69XFK		Foam	64	78	Worcester City & County	ND5 Hagley Rd-Halesowen-74
		Salvage			West Midlands Fire Service	F01 Dudley-78
		Tender				Damaged in RTA (66)-repaired
						Morris FG-HCB
						COMMER
RYX400		Hose	56	79	Worcester City & County	F27 Birmingham Rd Redditch 74
		Laying			Hereford & Worcester FB	27 Redditch
		Lorry				Q4-Superpoise-*HOS*
						LEYLAND
GLW428	MW-93	Turntable	42	64	Worcester City & County FB	1 Copenhagen Street
		Ladder	64		Rentokil Ltd	*TD7-Merryweather-100L*
GXA63		Turntable	43	69	FF23 Rugby (Warwickshire)	N26 Rugby Fire Station-?
	MW-105	Ladder			Worcester City & County FB	2 Kidderminster-64/1 Worcester
						Beaver TSC18-Merryweather-100L

Bibliography

Bentleys Directory archives

Berrows Newspaper Group, Hylton Road, Worcester

Billings Directory archives

Bromsgrove Messenger

Fire Service College Library, Moreton-in-Marsh, Gloucestershire

Fire magazine archives

Hereford & Worcester Fire Brigade, Media and Design Department

Kidderminster Library archives

Kidderminster *Shuttle Times & News*

Needle District Almanack

Norwich Union Fire Insurance Company archives (Aviva plc)

Redditch Indicator/Advertiser

Stourbridge Library archives

Surrey History Centre, Woking, Surrey. Photographic archives reproduced by
    permission of Transbus Dennis International Ltd and Surrey History Service

The Fireman Journal Archives

Worcester Records Office, County Hall

Worcester History Centre, Trinity Street (Vehicle Registration Records)

Worcester City and County Fire Brigade Chief Officers' Reports (1948-1974)

Other local titles published by Tempus

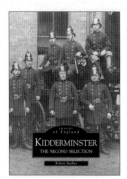

Kidderminster The Second Selection
ROBERT BARBER

This intriguing compilation of photographs provides a delightful insight into this Worcestershire town. The history of the town's great companies, both past and present, are explored including Brinton's Carpet Company, T. & A. Naylor, The Castle Motor Company, and the Sugar Factory which recently closed after seventy-seven years of production.
0 7524 2619 2

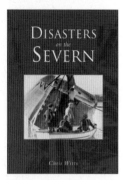

Disasters on the Severn
CHRIS WITTS

In *Disasters on the Severn*, Chris Witts, an experienced navigator of the river, has compiled a fascinating catalogue of such incidents. As well as recounting historical crises, he also tells of his personal experiences of difficulty, panic and loss on the river.
0 7524 2383 5

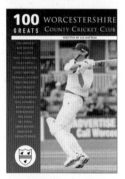

Worcestershire CCC 100 Greats
LES HATTON

Worcestershire celebrated 100 years of first-class cricket in 1999, but after the struggling days of the 1920s it is perhaps lucky that the club still survives at all. This volume celebrates Worcestershire's 100 greatest players and is compiled by Les Hatton, the club's statistician and editor of the ACS Second Eleven Annual, with a foreword by Tim Curtis.
0 7524 2194 8

Motoring Around Hereford, Worcester & The Welsh Marches
A.B. DEMAUS

This richly illustrated volume on motoring in Hereford, Worcester and the Welsh Marches shows the many uses that wheeled transport has been put to. There are bicycles, cars of all shapes, sizes and ages, lorries, steam traction engines as well as views of motor sport in the area. Covered in detail are local manufacturers such as Morgan, now one of the largest independent motor manufacturers left in Britain.
0 7524 2361 4

If you are interested in purchasing other books published by Tempus, or in case you have difficulty finding any Tempus books in your local bookshop, you can also place orders directly through our website
www.tempus-publishing.com